9/6

T. S. ELIOT

A STUDY OF HIS WRITINGS BY SEVERAL HANDS

T. S. ELIOT
A STUDY OF HIS WRITINGS BY SEVERAL HANDS

EDITED BY
B. RAJAN

FOCUS THREE

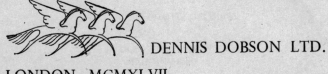

DENNIS DOBSON LTD.

LONDON · MCMXLVII

FIRST PUBLISHED IN GREAT BRITAIN IN 1947 BY
DENNIS DOBSON LIMITED
29 GREAT QUEEN STREET
KINGSWAY , LONDON WC2

PRINTED IN GREAT BRITAIN
in 12-pt. Perpetua

WHITEHILL (PRINTERS) LTD.
BIRMINGHAM

56/R

FOREWORD

This book, while including an essay on Mr Eliot's criticism, is intended chiefly to serve as a reasonably detailed introduction to his poetry. Hitherto readers desiring such an introduction have had to resort to Professor F. O. Matthiessen's *The Achievement of T. S. Eliot*; but this book, valuable as it is, was written ten years ago, and is moreover planned in such a way as to make a consecutive study of the poems impossible. The present volume, therefore, should go some way towards meeting a long-felt want.

In accordance with the trend of interest today in Mr Eliot's poetry, most space has been devoted to articles on the Quartets. But there are also studies of *Ash Wednesday*, *The Waste Land* and *Gerontion*.

The division of labour has been planned with some care to avoid overlapping and I should like to record my thanks to my contributors who have put up so patiently with my sometimes tyrannical demands. In addition I am grateful to Mr John Hayward for his encouragement and for valuable help with the bibliography, to Miss H. L. Gardner for reading and criticizing some of the essays, and to Professor Cleanth Brooks for several suggestions. The University of North Carolina Press have very kindly given permission for Professor Brooks' article to be reprinted. Miss H. L. Gardner's essay is a revised and augmented version, specially written for this volume, of an article which originally appeared in *New Writing and Daylight*. I am grateful to the proprietors of this periodical for permission to use material embodied in the earlier essay. The quotations from Mr. Eliot's works are reprinted by kind permission of Messrs. Faber & Faber Ltd.

B . R A J A N

Trinity College
Cambridge

CONTENTS

The Waste Land: An Analysis

TO VENTURE to write anything further on *The Waste Land*, particularly after the work of F. R. Leavis and F. O. Matthiessen, may call for some explanation and even apology. I am obviously indebted to both critics. The justification for such a commentary as this must be made primarily in terms of a difference of intention. Leavis is interested predominantly in Eliot's method of organization. One or two passages in the poem are treated in detail and are highly valuable for a knowledge of the 'meaning' of the poem, but the bulk of the poem does not receive this kind of examination. Moreover, I believe, Leavis makes some positive errors. Matthiessen examines more of the poem in detail, and, as far as it goes, his account is excellent. But the plan of his *Achievement of T. S. Eliot* does not allow for a consecutive examination either. He puts his finger on the basic theme, death-in-life, but I do not think that he has given it all the salience which it deserves.

I prefer not to raise here the question of how important it is for the reader of the poem to have an explicit intellectual account of the various symbols, and a logical account of their relationships. It may well be that such rationalization is no more than a scaffolding to be got out of the way before we contemplate the poem itself as a poem. But many readers (including myself) find the erection of such a scaffolding valuable—if not absolutely necessary—and if some readers will be tempted to lay more stress on the scaffolding than they properly should, there are perhaps still more readers who will be prevented from getting at the poem at all without the help of such a scaffolding. Furthermore, an interest attaches to Mr Eliot's own mental processes, and whereas Mr Matthiessen has quite properly warned us that Eliot's poetry cannot be read as autobiography, many of the symbols and ideas which occur in *The Waste Land* are ideas which are definitely central to Eliot's general intellectual position.

The basic symbol used, that of the waste land, is taken, of course, from Miss Jessie Weston's *From Ritual to Romance*. In the legends which she treats there, the land has been blighted by a curse. The crops do not grow, and the animals cannot reproduce. The plight of the land is summed up by, and connected with, the plight of the lord of the land, the Fisher King, who has been rendered impotent by maiming or sickness. The curse can only be removed by the appearance of a knight who will ask the meanings of the various symbols which are displayed to him in the castle. The shift in meaning from physical to spiritual sterility is easily made, and was, as a matter of fact, made in certain of the legends. A knowledge of this symbolism is, as Eliot has already pointed out, essential for an understanding of the poem.

Of hardly less importance to the reader, however, is a knowledge of Eliot's basic method. *The Waste Land* is built on a major contrast—a device which is a favourite of Eliot's and to be found in many of his poems, particularly his later poems. The contrast is between two kinds of life and two kinds of death. Life devoid of meaning is death; sacrifice, even the sacrificial death, may be life-giving, an awakening to life. The poem occupies itself to a great extent with this paradox, and with a number of variations on it.

Eliot has stated the matter quite explicitly himself in one of his essays. In his 'Baudelaire' he says:

One aphorism which has been especially noticed is the following: *la volupte unique et suprême de l'amour gît dans la certitude de faire le mal*. This means, I think, that Baudelaire has perceived that what distinguishes the relations of man and woman from the copulation of beasts is the knowledge of Good and Evil (of *moral* Good and Evil which are not natural Good and Bad or puritan Right and Wrong). Having an imperfect, vague romantic conception of Good, he was at least able to understand that the sexual act as evil is more dignified, less boring than as the natural, 'life-giving', cheery automatism of the modern world. . . . So far as we are human, what we do must be either evil or good; so far as we do evil or good, we are human; and it is better, in a paradoxical way, to do evil than to do nothing: at least, *we exist* [italics mine].

8

The Waste Land: An Analysis

The last statement is highly important for an understanding of
The Waste Land. The fact that men have lost the knowledge of
good and evil keeps them from being alive, and is the justification
for viewing the modern waste land as a realm in which people do
not even exist.

This theme is stated in the quotation which prefaces the poem.
The Sybil says: 'I wish to die'. Her statement has several possible
interpretations. For one thing, she is saying what the people who
inhabit the waste land are saying. But she also may be saying
what the speaker says in *The Journey of the Magi*, . . . 'this Birth
was/Hard and bitter agony for us, like Death, our death/ . . . I
should be glad of another death'.

I

The first section of 'The Burial of the Dead' develops the
theme of the attractiveness of death, or of the difficulty in rous-
ing oneself from the death in life in which the people of the
waste land live. Men are afraid to live in reality. April, the
month of rebirth, is not the most joyful season but the cruellest.
Winter at least kept us warm in forgetful snow. The idea is one
which Eliot has stressed elsewhere. Earlier in *Gerontion* he had
written

> *In the juvescence of the year*
> *Came Christ the tiger*
>
> .   .   .   .   .   .
>
> *The tiger springs in the new year. Us he devours.*

More lately, in *Murder in the Cathedral*, he has the chorus say

> *We do not wish anything to happen.*
> *Seven years we have lived quietly,*
> *Succeeded in avoiding notice,*
> *Living and partly living.*

And in another passage: 'Now I fear disturbance of the quiet
seasons'. Men dislike to be aroused from their death-in-life.

The first part of 'The Burial of the Dead' introduces this
theme through a sort of reverie on the part of the protagonist—a
reverie in which speculation on life glides off into memory of an
actual conversation in the Hofgarten and back into speculation
again. The function of the conversation is to establish to some

9

extent the class and character of the protagonist. The reverie is resumed with line 19.

> *What are the roots that clutch, what branches grow*
> *Out of this stony rubbish?*

The protagonist answers for himself:

> *Son of man,*
> *You cannot say, or guess, for you know only*
> *A heap of broken images, where the sun beats,*
> *And the dead tree gives no shelter, the cricket no relief,*
> *And the dry stone no sound of water.*

In this passage there are references to Ezekiel and to Ecclesiastes, and these references indicate what it is that men no longer know: the passage referred to in, Ezekiel ii, pictures a world thoroughly secularized:

> 1. And he said unto me, Son of man, stand upon thy feet, and I will speak unto thee. 2. And the spirit entered into me when he spake unto me, and set me upon my feet, that I heard him that spake unto me. 3. And he said unto me, Son of man, I send thee to the children of Israel, to a rebellious nation that hath rebelled against me: they and their fathers have transgressed against me, even unto this very day.

The following passage from Ecclesiastes xii, is not only referred to in this passage; a reference to it also is evidently made in the nightmare vision of Section V of the poem:

> 1. Remember now thy Creator in the days of thy youth, while the evil days come not, nor the years draw nigh, when thou shalt say, I have no pleasure in them; 2. While the sun, or the light, or the moon, or the stars, be not darkened, nor the clouds return after the rain: 3. In the day when the keepers of the house shall tremble, and the strong men shall bow themselves, and the grinders cease because they are few, and those that look out of the windows be darkened, 4. And the doors shall be shut in the streets, when the sound of the grinding is low, and he shall rise up at the voice of the bird, and all the daughters of musick shall be brought low; 5. Also when they shall be afraid of that which is high, and fears shall be in the way, and the almond tree shall flourish, and the grasshopper shall be a burden, *and desire shall fail* [italics mine]: because man goeth to his long home, and the mourners go about the streets: 6. Or ever the silver cord be loosed, or the golden bowl be broken, or the pitcher be broken at the fountain, or the wheel broken at the cistern. 7. Then shall the dust return to the earth as it was: and the spirit shall return unto God who gave it.

The Waste Land: An Analysis

8. Vanity of vanities, saith the preacher; all is vanity.

The next section which begins with the scrap of song quoted
from Wagner (perhaps another item in the reverie of the protagonist), states the opposite half of the paradox which underlies
the poem: namely, that life at its highest moments of meaning
and intensity resembles death. The song from Act I of Wagner's
Tristan und Isolde, 'Frisch weht der Wind', is sung in the opera
by a young sailor aboard the ship which is bringing Isolde to
Cornwall. The '*Irisch kind*' of the song does not properly apply to
Isolde at all. The song is merely one of happy and naïve love. It
brings to the mind of the protagonist an experience of love—
the vision of the hyacinth girl as she came back from the
hyacinth garden. The poet says

> . . . *my eyes failed, I was neither*
> *Living nor dead, and I knew nothing,*
> *Looking into the heart of light, the silence.*

The line which immediately follows this passage, 'Oed' und leer
das Meer', seems at first to be simply an extension of the last
figure: that is, 'Empty and wide the sea [of silence]'. The line,
however, as a matter of fact, makes an ironic contrast; for the
line as it occurs in Act III of the opera, is the reply of the
watcher who reports to the wounded Tristan that Isolde's ship is
nowhere in sight; the sea is empty. And, though the '*Irisch kind*'
of the first quotation is not Isolde, the reader familiar with the
opera will apply it to Isolde when he comes to the line 'Oed'
und leer das Meer'. For the question in the song is in essence
Tristan's question in Act III: My Irish child, where dwellest
thou? The two quotations from the opera which frame the
ecstasy-of-love passage thus take on a new meaning in the
altered context. In the first, love is happy: the boat rushes on
with a fair wind behind it. In the second, love is absent; the sea
is wide and empty. And the last quotation reminds us that even
love cannot exist in the waste land.

The next passage, that in which Madame Sosostris figures,
calls for further reference to Miss Weston's book. As Miss
Weston has shown, the Tarot cards were originally used to
determine the event of the highest importance to the people,
the rising of the waters. Madame Sosostris has fallen a long way

from the high function of her predecessors. She is engaged merely in vulgar fortune-telling—is merely one item in a generally vulgar civilization. But the symbols of the Tarot pack are still unchanged. The various characters are still inscribed on the cards, and she is reading in reality, though she does not know it, the fortune of the protagonist. She finds that his card is that of the drowned Phœnician Sailor, and so she warns him against death by water, not realizing any more than do the other inhabitants of the modern waste land that the way into life may be by death itself. The drowned Phœnician Sailor is a type of the fertility god whose image was thrown into the sea annually as a symbol of the death of summer. As for the other figures in the pack: Belladonna, the Lady of the Rocks, is woman in the waste land. The man with three staves, Eliot says he associates rather arbitrarily with the Fisher King. The term 'arbitrarily' indicates that we are not to attempt to find a logical connection here.

The Hanged Man, who represents the hanged god of Frazer (including the Christ), Eliot states in a note, is associated with the hooded figure who appears in 'What the Thunder Said'. That he is hooded accounts for Madame Sosostris' inability to see him; or rather, here again the palaver of the modern fortune-teller is turned to new and important account by the poet's shifting the matter into a new and serious context. The Wheel and the one-eyed merchant will be discussed later.

After the Madame Sosostris passage, Eliot proceeds to complicate his symbols for the sterility and unreality of the modern waste land by associating it with Baudelaire's *fourmillante cité* and with Dante's Limbo. The passages already quoted from Eliot's essay on Baudelaire will indicate one of the reasons why Baudelaire's lines are evoked here. In Baudelaire's city, dream and reality seem to mix, and it is interesting that Eliot in *The Hollow Men* refers to this same realm of death-in-life as 'death's dream kingdom' in contradistinction to 'death's other kingdom'.

The references to Dante are most important. The line, 'I had not thought death had undone so many', is taken from the Third Canto of the *Inferno*; the line, 'Sighs, short and infrequent, were exhaled', from the Fourth Canto. Mr Matthiessen has already pointed out that the Third Canto deals with Dante's Limbo which is occupied by those who on earth had 'lived without praise or blame'. They share this abode with the angels,

'Who were not rebels, nor were faithful to God, but were for themselves'. They exemplify almost perfectly the secular attitude which dominates the modern world. Their grief, according to Dante, arises from the fact that they 'have no hope of death; and their blind life is so debased, that they are envious of every other lot'. But though they may not hope for death, Dante calls them 'these wretches who never were alive'. The people who are treated in the Fourth Canto are those who lived virtuously but who died before the proclamation of the Gospel—they are the unbaptized. This completes the categories of people who inhabit the modern waste land: those who are secularized and those who have no knowledge of the faith. Without a faith their life is in reality a death. To repeat the sentence from Eliot previously quoted: 'So far as we do evil or good, we are human; and it is better, in a paradoxical way, to do evil than to do nothing: at least, we exist.'

The Dante and Baudelaire references, then, come to the same thing as the allusion to the waste land of the medieval legends; and these various allusions drawn from widely differing sources enrich the comment on the modern city so that it becomes 'unreal' on a number of levels: as seen through 'the brown fog of a winter dawn'; as the medieval waste land and Dante's Limbo and Baudelaire's Paris are unreal.

The reference to Stetson stresses again the connection between the modern London of the poem and Dante's hell. After the statement, 'I could never have believed death had undone so many', follow the words 'After I had distinguished some among them, I saw and knew the shade of him who made, through cowardice, the great refusal'. The protagonist, like Dante, sees among the inhabitants of the contemporary waste land one whom he recognizes. (The name 'Stetson' I take to have no ulterior significance. It is merely an ordinary name such as might be borne by the friend one might see in a crowd in a great city.) Mylae, as Mr Matthiessen has pointed out to us, is the name of a battle between the Romans and the Carthaginians in the Punic War. The Punic War was a trade war—might be considered a rather close parallel to the war of 1914-18. At any rate, it is plain that Eliot in having the protagonist address the friend in a London street as one who was with him in the Punic War rather than as one who was with him in the World War is making the point that all the wars are one war; all experience, one experience. As Eliot put the idea in *Murder in the Cathedral*:

> *We do not know very much of the future*
> *Except that from generation to generation*
> *The same things happen again and again.*

I am not sure that Leavis and Matthiessen are correct in inferring that the line, 'That corpse you planted last year in your garden', refers to the attempt to bury a memory. But whether or not this is true, the line certainly refers also to the buried god of the old fertility rites. It also is to be linked with the earlier passage—'What are the roots that clutch, what branches grow', etc. This allusion to the buried god will account for the ironical, almost taunting tone of the passage. The burial of the dead is now a sterile planting—without hope. But the advice to 'keep the Dog far hence', in spite of the tone, is, I believe, well taken and serious. The passage in Webster goes as follows

> *O keep the wolf far hence, that's foe to men,*
> *Or with his nails he'll dig it up again.*

Why does Eliot turn the wolf into a dog? And why does he reverse the point of importance from the animal's normal hostility to men to its friendliness? If, as some critics have suggested, he is merely interested in making a reference to Webster's darkest play, why alter the line? I am inclined to take the Dog (the capital letter is Eliot's) as Humanitarianism and the related philosophies which in their concern for man extirpate the supernatural—dig up the corpse of the buried god and thus prevent the rebirth of life. For the general idea, see Eliot's essay, 'The Humanism of Irving Babbitt'.

The last line of 'The Burial of the Dead'—'You! hypocrite lecteur!—mon semblable,—mon frère!'—the quotation from Baudelaire, completes the universalization of Stetson begun by the reference to Mylae. Stetson is every man, including the reader and Mr Eliot himself.

II

If 'The Burial of the Dead' gives the general abstract statement on the situation, the second part of *The Waste Land*, 'A Game of Chess', gives a more concrete illustration. The easiest contrast in this section—and one which may easily blind the casual reader to a continued emphasis on the contrast between the two kinds of life, or the two kinds of death, already commented on—is the contrast between life in a rich and magnificent setting, and life in the low and vulgar setting of a London pub. But both scenes, however antithetical they may appear superficially, are scenes taken from the contemporary waste land. In both of them life has lost its meaning.

I am particularly indebted to Mr Allen Tate's brilliant comment on the first part of this section. To quote from him, 'the woman . . . is, I believe, the symbol of man at the present time. He is surrounded by the grandeurs of the past, but he does not participate in them; they don't sustain him'. And to quote from another section of his commentary: 'The rich experience of the great tradition depicted in the room receives a violent shock in contrast with a game that symbolizes the inhuman abstraction of the modern mind'. Life has no meaning; history has no meaning; there is no answer to the question: 'What shall we ever do?' The only thing that has meaning is the abstract game which they are to play, a game in which the meaning is assigned and arbitrary, meaning by convention only—in short, a game of chess.

This interpretation will account in part for the pointed reference to Cleopatra in the first lines of the section. But there is, I believe, a further reason for the poet's having compared the lady to Cleopatra. The queen in Shakespeare's drama—'Age cannot wither her, nor custom stale/Her infinite variety'—is perhaps the extreme exponent of love for love's sake—the feminine member of the pair of lovers who threw away an empire for love. But the infinite variety of the life of the woman in 'A Game of Chess' *has* been staled. There is indeed no variety at all, and love simply does not exist. The function of the sudden change in the description of the carvings and paintings in the room from the heroic and magnificent to the characterization of the rest of them as 'other withered stumps of time' is obvious. But the reference to Philomela is particularly important, for Philomela, it seems to me, is one of the major symbols of the poem.

Miss Weston points out that a section of one of the Grail manuscripts, which is apparently intended as a gloss of the Grail story, tells how the court of the rich Fisher King was withdrawn from the knowledge of men when certain of the maidens who frequented the shrine were raped and had their golden cups taken from them. The curse on the land follows from this act. Miss Weston conjectures that this may be a statement, in the form of parable, of the violation of the older mysteries which were probably once celebrated openly, but were later forced underground into secrecy. Whether or not Mr Eliot intends a reference to this passage, the violation of a woman makes a very good symbol of the process of secularization. John Crowe Ransom makes the point very neatly for us in his *God Without Thunder*. Love is the æsthetic of sex; lust is the science. Love implies a deferring of the satisfaction of the desire; it implies even a certain asceticism and a ritual. Lust drives forward urgently and scientifically to the immediate extirpation of the desire. Our contemporary waste land is in a large part the result of our scientific attitude—of our complete secularization. Needless to say, lust defeats its own ends. The portrayal of 'The change of Philomel, by the barbarous king' is a fitting commentary on the scene which it ornaments. The waste land of the legend came in this way—the modern waste land has come in this way.

That this view is not mere fine-spun ingenuity is borne out somewhat by the change of tense which Eliot employs here and which Mr Edmund Wilson has commented upon: 'And still she cried, and still the world pursues'. Apparently the 'world' partakes in the barbarous king's action, and still partakes in that action.

To 'dirty ears' the nightingale's song is not that which filled all the desert with inviolable voice—it is 'jug, jug'. Edmund Wilson has pointed out that the rendition of the bird's song here represents not merely the Elizabethan neutral notation of the bird's song, but carries associations of the ugly and coarse. The passage is therefore one of many instances of Eliot's device of using something which in one context is innocent but in another context becomes loaded with a special meaning.

The Philomela passage has another importance, however. If it is a commentary on how the waste land became waste, it also repeats the theme of the death which is the door to life—the theme of the dying god. The raped woman becomes transformed through suffering into the nightingale; through the violation comes the 'inviolable voice'. The thesis that suffering is action,

The Waste Land: An Analysis

and that out of suffering comes poetry is a favourite one of Eliot's. For example, 'Shakespeare, too, was occupied with the struggle—which alone constitutes life for a poet—to transmute his personal and private agonies into something rich and strange, something universal and impersonal'. Consider also his statement with reference to Baudelaire: 'Indeed, in his way of suffering is already a kind of presence of the supernatural and of the superhuman. He rejects always the purely natural and the purely human; in other words, he is neither "naturalist" nor "humanist".' The theme of the life which is death is stated specifically in the conversation between the man and the woman. She asks the question 'Are you alive, or not?' and this time we are sufficiently prepared by the Dante references in 'The Burial of the Dead' for the statement here to bear a special meaning. (She also asks 'Is there nothing in your head?' He is one of the Hollow Men—'headpiece stuffed with straw'.) These people, as people in the waste land, know nothing, see nothing, do not even live.

But the protagonist, after this reflection that in the waste land of modern life even death is sterile—'I think we are in rats' alley/Where the dead men lost their bones'—remembers a death which was not sterile, remembers a death that was transformed into something rich and strange, the death described in the song from *The Tempest*—'Those are pearls that were his eyes'.

The reference to this section of *The Tempest* is, like the Philomela reference, one of Eliot's major symbols. We are to meet it twice more, in later sections of the poem. Some more general comment on it is therefore appropriate here. The song, one remembers, was sung by Ariel in luring Ferdinand, Prince of Naples, on to meet Miranda, and thus to find love, and through this love, to effect the regeneration and deliverance of all the people on the island. Ferdinand says of the song.

> The ditty doth remember my drowned father.
> This is no mortal business, nor no sound
> That the earth owes. . . .

The allusion is an extremely interesting example of the device of Eliot's already commented upon, that of taking an item from one context and shifting it into another in which it assumes a new and powerful meaning. This description of a death which is a

17

portal into a realm of the rich and strange—a death which becomes a sort of birth—assumes in the mind of the protagonist an
association with that of the drowned god whose effigy was
thrown into the water as a symbol of the death of the fruitful
powers of nature but which was taken out of the water as a
symbol of the revivified god. (See *From Ritual to Romance*.) The
passage therefore represents the perfect antithesis to the passage
in 'The Burial of the Dead': 'That corpse you planted last year in
your garden', etc. It also, as we have already pointed out, finds
its antithesis in the sterile and unfruitful death 'in rats' alley'
just commented upon. (We shall find that this contrast between
the death in rats' alley and the death in *The Tempest* is made again
in 'The Fire Sermon'.)

We have yet to treat the relation of the title of the section,
'A Game of Chess', to Middleton's play, *Women beware Women*,
from which the game of chess is taken. In the play, the game is
used as a device to keep the widow occupied while her daughter-
in-law is being seduced. The seduction amounts almost to a rape,
and in a *double entendre* the rape is actually described in terms of
the game. We have one more connection with the Philomela
symbol therefore. The abstract game is being used in the contemporary waste land, as in the play, to cover up a rape and is a
description of the rape itself.

In the second part of 'A Game of Chess' we are given a picture
of spiritual emptiness, but this time, at the other end of the
social scale, as reflected in the talk between two cockney women
in a London pub. The account here is straightforward enough
and the only matter which calls for comment is the line spoken
by Ophelia in *Hamlet* which ends the passage. Ophelia, too, was
very much concerned about love, the theme of conversation of
the two ladies. As a matter of fact, she was in very much the
same position as that of the woman who has been the topic of
conversation between the two good ladies we have just heard.
She had remarked too once that

> Young men will do't, if they come to't!
> By cock, they are to blame.

And her poetry (including the line quoted from her here), like
Philomela's, had come out of suffering. I think that we are
probably to look for the relevance of the allusion to her in some

such matter as this rather than in an easy satiric contrast between Elizabethan glories and modern sordidness. After all (in spite of the Marxists) Eliot's objection to the present world is not merely the sentimental one that this happens to be the twentieth century after Christ and not the seventeenth.

III

'The Fire Sermon' makes much use of several of the symbols already developed. The fire is the sterile burning of lust, and the section is a sermon, although a sermon by example only. This section of the poem also contains some of the most easily apprehended uses of literary allusion. The poem opens on a vision of the modern river. In Spenser's *Prothalamion* the scene described is also a river scene at London, and it is dominated by nymphs and their paramours, and the nymphs are preparing for a bridal. The contrast between Spenser's scene and its twentieth-century equivalent is jarring. The paramours are now 'the loitering heirs of city directors', and, as for the bridals of Spenser's Elizabethan maidens, in the stanzas which follow we learn a great deal about those. At the end of the section the speech of the third of the Thames-nymphs summarizes the whole matter for us.

The waters of the Thames are also associated with those of Leman—the poet in the contemporary waste land is in a sort of Babylonian Captivity.

The castle of the Fisher King was always located on the banks of a river or on the sea shore. The title 'Fisher King', Miss Weston shows, originates from the use of the fish as a fertility or life symbol. This meaning, however, was often forgotten, and so the title in many of the later Grail romances is accounted for by describing the king as fishing. Eliot uses the reference to fishing for reverse effect. The reference to fishing is part of the realistic detail of the scene—'While I was fishing in the dull canal'. But to the reader who knows the Weston references, the reference is to that of the Fisher King of the Grail legends. The protagonist is the maimed and impotent king of the legends.

Eliot proceeds now to tie the waste-land symbol to that of *The Tempest*, by quoting one of the lines spoken by Ferdinand, Prince of Naples, which occurs just before Ariel's song, 'Full Fathom

Five', is heard. But he alters the passage from *The Tempest* somewhat, writing not, 'Weeping again the king my father's wreck', but

> *Musing upon the king my brother's wreck*
> *And on the king my father's death before him.*

It is possible that the alteration has been made to bring the
account taken from *The Tempest* into accord with the situation in
the Percival stories. In Wolfram von Eschenbach's *Parzival*, for
instance, Trevrezent, the hermit, is the brother of the Fisher
King, Anfortas. He tells Parzival, 'His name all men know as
Anfortas, and I weep for him evermore'. Their father, Frimutel,
is of course, dead.

The protagonist in the poem, then, imagines himself not only
in the situation of Ferdinand in *The Tempest* but also in that of one
of the characters in the Grail legend; and the wreck, to be
applied literally in the first instance, applies metaphorically in
the second.

After the lines from *The Tempest*, appears again the image of a
sterile death from which no life comes, the bones, 'rattled by
the rat's foot only, year to year'. (The collocation of this figure
with the vision of the death by water in Ariel's song has already
been commented on. The lines quoted from *The Tempest* come
just before the song.)

The allusion to Marvell's *To His Coy Mistress* is of course one
of the easiest allusions in the poem. Instead of 'Time's winged
chariot' the poet hears 'the sound of horns and motors' of contemporary London. But the passage has been further complicated.
The reference has been combined with an allusion to Day's
Parliament of Bees. 'Time's winged chariot' of Marvell has not
only been changed to the modern automobile; Day's 'sound of
horns and hunting' has changed to the horns of the motors. And
Actæon will not be brought face to face with Diana, goddess of
chastity; Sweeney, type of the vulgar bourgeois, is to be brought
to Mrs Porter, hardly a type of chastity. The reference in the
ballad to the feet 'washed in soda water' reminds the poet
ironically of another sort of foot-washing, the sound of the
children singing in the dome heard at the ceremony of the foot-
washing which precedes the restoration of the wounded Anfortas
(the Fisher King) by Parzival and the taking away of the curse
from the waste land. The quotation thus completes the allusion

to the Fisher King commenced in line 189—'While I was fishing in the dull canal'.

The pure song of the children also reminds the poet of the song of the nightingale which we have heard in 'The Game of Chess'. The recapitulation of symbols is continued with a repetition of 'Unreal city' and with the reference to the one-eyed merchant.

Mr Eugenides, the Smyrna merchant, is the one-eyed merchant mentioned by Madame Sosostris. The fact that the merchant is one-eyed apparently means in Madame Sosostris's speech no more than that the merchant's face on the card is shown in profile. But Eliot applies the term to Mr Eugenides for a totally different effect. The defect corresponds somewhat to Madame Sosostris's bad cold. The Syrian merchants, we learn from Miss Weston's book, were, with slaves and soldiers, the principal carriers of the mysteries which lie at the core of the Grail legends. But in the modern world we find both the representatives of the Tarot divining and the mystery cults in decay. What he carries on his back and what the fortune-teller was forbidden to see is evidently the knowledge of the mysteries (although Mr Eugenides himself is hardly likely to be more aware of it than Madame Sosostris is aware of the importance of her function). Mr Eugenides, in terms of his former function, ought to be inviting the protagonist to an initiation into the esoteric cult which holds the secret of life, but on the realistic surface of the poem, in his invitation to 'a weekend at the Metropole' he is really inviting him to a homosexual debauch. The homosexuality is 'secret' and now a 'cult', but a very different cult from that which Mr Eugenides ought to represent. The end of the new cult is not life but, ironically, sterility.

In the modern waste land, however, even the relation between man and woman is also sterile. The incident between the typist and the carbuncular young man is a picture of 'love' so exclusively and practically pursued that it is not love at all. The scene, as Allen Tate puts it, is one of our most terrible insights into Western civilization. The tragic chorus to the scene is Tiresias, into whom perhaps Mr Eugenides may be said to modulate, Tiresias, the historical 'expert' on the relation between the sexes.

The allusions to Sappho's lines and to Goldsmith's made in

21

this passage need little comment. The hour of evening, which in Sappho's poem brings rest to all and brings the sailor home, brings the typist to her travesty of home—'On the divan . . . at night her bed'—and brings the carbuncular young man, the meeting with whom ends not in peace but in sterile burning.

The reminiscence of the lines from Goldsmith's song in the description of the young woman's actions after the departure of her lover gives concretely and ironically the utter breakdown of traditional standards.

It is the music of her gramophone which the protagonist hears 'creep by' him 'upon the waters'. Far from the music which Ferdinand heard bringing him to Miranda and love, it is, one is tempted to think, the music of 'O O O O that Shakespeherian Rag' of 'A Game of Chess'.

But the protagonist says that he *sometimes* hears 'The pleasant whining of a mandoline'. Significantly enough, it is the music of the fishmen (the fish again as a life symbol) and it comes from beside a church (though—if this is not to rely too much on Eliot's note—the church has been marked for destruction). Life on Lower Thames Street, if not on the Strand, still has meaning as it cannot have meaning for either the typist or the rich woman of 'A Game of Chess'.

The song of the Thames-daughters brings us back to the opening section of 'The Fire Sermon' again, and once more we have to do with the river and the river-nymphs. Indeed, the typist incident is framed by the two river-nymph scenes.

The connection of the river-nymphs with the Rhine-daughters of Wagner's *Gotterdammerung* is easily made. In the passage in Wagner's opera to which Eliot refers in his note, the opening of Act III, the Rhine-daughters bewail the loss of the beauty of the Rhine occasioned by the theft of the gold, and then beg Siegfried to give them back the Ring made from this gold, finally threatening him with death if he does not give it up. Like the Thames-daughters they too have been violated; and like the maidens mentioned in the Grail legend, the violation has brought a curse on gods and men. The first of the songs depicts the modern river, soiled with oil and tar. (Compare also with the description of the river in the first part of 'The Fire Sermon'.) The second song depicts the Elizabethan river, also evoked in the first part of 'The Fire Sermon'. (Leicester and Elizabeth ride upon it in a barge of state. Incidentally, Spenser's *Pro-thalamion*, from which quotation is made in the first part of 'The Fire Sermon', mentions Leicester as having formerly lived in the house which forms the setting of that poem.)

In this second song there is also a definite allusion to the passage in *Antony and Cleopatra* already referred to in the opening line of 'A Game of Chess'.

> *Beating oars*
> *The stern was formed*
> *A gilded shell.*

And if we still have any doubt of the allusion, Eliot's note on the passage with its reference to the 'barge' and 'poop' should settle the matter. We have already commented on the earlier allusion to Cleopatra as the prime example of love for love's sake. The symbol bears something of the same meaning here, and the note which Eliot supplies does something to reinforce the 'Cleopatra' aspect of Elizabeth. Elizabeth in the presence of the Spaniard De Quadra, though negotiations were going on for a Spanish marriage, 'went so far that Lord Robert at last said, as I [De Quadra was a bishop] was on the spot there was no reason why they should not be married if the queen pleased'. The passage has a sort of double function. It reinforces the general contrast between Elizabethan magnificence and modern sordidness: in the Elizabethan age love for love's sake had some meaning and therefore some magnificence. But the passage gives something of an opposed effect too: the same sterile love, emptiness of love, obtained in this period too: Elizabeth and the Typist are alike as well as different.

The third Thames-daughter's song depicts another sordid 'love' affair, and unites the themes of the first two songs. It begins 'Trams and *dusty* trees'. With it we are definitely in the waste land again. Pia, whose words she echoes in saying 'High-bury bore me. Richmond and Kew/Undid me' was in Purgatory and had hope. The woman speaking here has no hope—she too is in the Inferno: 'I can connect/Nothing with nothing'. She has just completed, floating down the river in the canoe, what Eliot has described in *Murder in the Cathedral* as

> . . . the effortless journey, to the empty land

> *Where the soul is no longer deceived, for there are no objects, no tones,*

Where those who were men can no longer turn the mind
To distraction, delusion, escape into dream, pretence,
No colours, no forms to distract, to divert the soul
From seeing itself, foully united forever, nothing with nothing,
Nor what we call death, but what beyond death is not death. . . .

Now, 'on Margate sands', like the Hollow Men, she stands 'on this beach of the tumid river'.

The songs of the three Thames-daughters, as a matter of fact, epitomize this whole section of the poem. With reference to the quotations from St Augustine and Buddha at the end of 'The Fire Sermon' Eliot states that 'The collocation of these two representatives of eastern and western asceticism, as the culmination of this part of the poem, is not an accident'.

It is certainly not an accident. The moral of all the incidents which we have been witnessing is that there must be an asceticism—something to check the drive of desire. The wisdom of the East and the West comes to the same thing on this point. Moreover, the image which both St Augustine and Buddha use for lust is fire. What we have witnessed in the various scenes of 'The Fire Sermon' is the sterile burning of lust. Modern man, freed from all restraints, in his cultivation of experience for experience's sake burns, but not with a 'hard and gemlike flame'. One ought not to pound the point home in this fashion, but to see that the imagery of this section of the poem furnishes illustrations leading up to 'The Fire Sermon' is the necessary requirement for feeling the force of the brief allusions here at the end to Buddha and St Augustine.

IV

Whatever the specific meaning of the symbols, the general function of the section, 'Death by Water', is readily apparent. The section forms a contrast with 'The Fire Sermon' which precedes it—a contrast between the symbolism of fire and that of water. Also readily apparent is its force as a symbol of surrender and relief through surrender.

Some specific connections can be made, however. The drowned Phœnician Sailor recalls the drowned god of the fertility cults. Miss Weston tells that each year at Alexandria an effigy of the head of the god was thrown into the water as a symbol of the death of the powers of nature, and that this head was carried by the current to Byblos where it was taken out of the water and exhibited as a symbol of the reborn god.

Moreover, the Phœnician Sailor is a merchant—'Forgot . . . the profit and loss'. The vision of the drowned sailor gives a statement of the message which the Syrian merchants originally brought to Britain and which the Smyrna merchant, unconsciously and by ironical negatives, has brought. One of Eliot's notes states that the 'merchant . . . melts into the Phœnician Sailor, and the latter is not wholly distinct from Ferdinand Prince of Naples'. The death by water would seem to be equated with the death described in Ariel's song in *The Tempest*. There is a definite difference in the tone of the description of this death—'A current under sea/Picked his bones in whispers', as compared with the 'other' death—'bones cast in a little low dry garret,/Rattled by the rat's foot only, year to year'.

Farther than this it would not be safe to go, but one may point out that whirling (the whirlpool here, the Wheel of Madame Sosostris' palaver) is one of Eliot's symbols frequently used in other poems (*Ash Wednesday*, *Gerontion*, *Murder in the Cathedral*, and *Burnt Norton*) to denote the temporal world. And one may point out, the following passage from *Ash Wednesday*:

> *Although I do not hope to* turn *again*
>
> .   .   .   .   .
>
> *Wavering between the* profit and the loss
> *In this brief transit where the dreams cross*
> *The dreamcrossed twilight* between birth and dying.

At least, with a kind of hindsight, one may suggest that Section IV gives an instance of the conquest of death and time—the 'perpetual recurrence of determined seasons', the 'world of spring and autumn, birth and dying'—through death itself.

V

The reference to the 'torchlight red on sweaty faces' and to the 'frosty silence in the gardens' obviously associates, as we have already pointed out, Christ in Gethsemane with the other hanged gods. The god has now died, and in referring to this, the basic theme finds another strong restatement:

> He who was living is now dead
> We who were living are now dying
> With a little patience

The poet does not say 'We who *are* living'. It is 'We who *were* living'. It is the death-in-life of Dante's Limbo. Life in the full sense has been lost.

The passage on the sterility of the waste land and the lack of water which follows, provides for the introduction later of two highly important passages:

> There is not even silence in the mountains
> But dry sterile thunder without rain

—lines which look forward to the introduction later of 'what the thunder said' when the thunder, no longer sterile, but bringing rain speaks.

The second of these passages is, 'There is not even solitude in the mountains', which looks forward to the reference to the Journey to Emmaus theme a few lines later: 'Who is the third who walks always beside you?' The god has returned, has risen, but the travellers cannot tell whether it is really he, or mere illusion induced by their delirium.

The parallelism between the 'hooded' figure who walks 'always . . . beside you', and the 'hooded hordes' is another instance of the sort of parallelism that is really a contrast, one of the type of which Eliot is fond. In the first case, the figure is indistinct because spiritual; in the second, the hooded hordes are indistinct because completely *unspiritual*—they are the people of the waste land—

> Shape without form, shade without colour,
> Paralysed force, gesture without motion

—to take two lines from 'The Hollow Men', where the people of the waste land once more appear. Or to take another line from the same poem, perhaps their hoods are the 'deliberate disguises' which the Hollow Men, the people of the waste land, wear.

Eliot, as his notes tell us, has particularly connected the description here with the 'decay of eastern Europe'. The hordes represent then the general waste land of the modern world with a special application to the break-up of Eastern Europe, the region with which the fertility cults were especially connected and in which to-day the traditional values are thoroughly discredited. The cities, Jerusalem, Athens, Alexandria, Vienna, like the London of the first section of the poem, are 'unreal', and for the same reason.

The passage which immediately follows develops the unreality into nightmare, but it is a nightmare vision which is not only an extension of the passage beginning, 'What is the city over the mountains'—in it appear other figures from earlier in the poem: the lady of 'A Game of Chess' who, surrounded by the glory of history and art sees no meaning in either and threatens to rush out into the street 'With my hair down, so', has here let down her hair and fiddles 'whisper music on those strings'. One remembers in 'A Game of Chess' that it was the woman's hair that spoke:

> . . . her hair
> Spread out in fiery points
> Glowed into words, then would be savagely still.

The hair has been immemorially a symbol of fertility, and Miss Weston and Frazer mention sacrifices of hair in order to aid the fertility god.

As we have pointed out earlier in dealing with 'The Burial of the Dead', this whole passage is to be connected with the twelfth chapter of Ecclesiastes. The doors 'of mudcracked houses', and the cisterns in this passage are to be found in Ecclesiastes, and the woman fiddling music from her hair is one of 'the daughters of music' brought low. The towers and bells from the Elizabeth and Leicester passage of 'The Fire Sermon' also appear here, but the towers are upside down, and the bells, far from pealing for an actual occasion or ringing the hours, are 'reminiscent'. The civilization is breaking up.

The 'violet light' also deserves comment. In 'The Fire Sermon' it is twice mentioned as the 'violet hour', and there it has little more than a physical meaning. It is a description of the hour of twilight. Here it indicates the twilight of the civilization, but it is perhaps something more. Violet is one of the liturgical colours of the Church. It symbolizes repentance and it is the colour of baptism. The visit to the Perilous Chapel, according to

27

Miss Weston, was an initiation—that is, a baptism. In the nightmare vision, the bats wear baby faces.

The horror built up in this passage is a proper preparation for the passage on the Perilous Chapel which follows it. The journey has not been merely an agonized walk in the desert, though it is that, or merely the journey after the god has died and hope has been lost; it is also the journey to the Perilous Chapel of the Grail story. In Miss Weston's account, the Chapel was part of the ritual, and was filled with horrors to test the candidate's courage. In some stories the perilous cemetery is also mentioned. Eliot has used both: 'Over the tumbled graves, about the chapel'. In many of the Grail stories the Chapel was haunted by demons.

The cock in the folk-lore of many peoples is regarded as the bird whose voice chases away the powers of evil. It is significant that it is after his crow that the flash of lightning comes and the 'damp gust/Bringing rain'. It is just possible that the cock has a connection also with *The Tempest* symbols. The first song which Ariel sings to Ferdinand as he sits 'Weeping again the king my father's wreck' ends

> The strain of strutting chanticleer,
> Cry, cock-a-doodle-doo.

The next stanza is the 'Full Fathom Five' song which Eliot has used as a vision of life gained through death. If this relation holds, here we have an extreme instance of an allusion, in itself innocent, forced into serious meaning through transference to a new context.

As Miss Weston has shown, the fertility cults go back to a very early period and are recorded in Sanskrit legends. Eliot has been continually in the poem linking up the Christian doctrine with the beliefs of as many peoples as he can. Here he goes back to the very beginnings of Aryan culture, and tells the rest of the story of the rain's coming, not in terms of the setting already developed but in its earliest form. The passage is thus a perfect parallel in method to the passage in 'The Burial of the Dead'.

> You who were with me in the ships at Mylæ!
> That corpse you planted last year in your garden. . . .

The use of Sanskrit in what the thunder says is thus accounted for. In addition, there is of course a more obvious reason for casting what the thunder said into Sanskrit here: onomatopœia.

The comments on the three statements of the thunder imply an acceptance of them. The protagonist answers the first question, 'What have we given?' with the statement:

> The awful daring of a moment's surrender
> Which an age of prudence can never retract
> By this, and this only, we have existed.

Here the larger meaning is stated in terms which imply the sexual meaning. Man cannot be absolutely self-regarding. Even the propagation of the race—even mere 'existence'—calls for such a surrender. Living calls for—see the passage already quoted from Eliot's essay on Baudelaire—belief in something more than 'life'.

The comment on *dayadhvam* (sympathize) is obviously connected with the foregoing passage. The surrender to something outside the self is an attempt (whether on the sexual level or some other) to transcend one's essential isolation. The passage gathers up the symbols previously developed in the poem just as the foregoing passage reflects, though with a different implication, the numerous references to sex made earlier in the poem. For example, the woman in the first part of 'A Game of Chess' has also heard the key turn in the door, and confirms her prison by thinking of the key:

> Speak to me. Why do you never speak. Speak.
> What are you thinking of? What thinking? What?
> I never know what you are thinking. Think.

The third statement made by the thunder, *damyata* (control) follows the logical condition for control, sympathy. The figure of the boat catches up the figure of control already given in 'Death by Water'—'O you who turn the wheel and look to windward'—and from 'The Burial of the Dead' the figure of happy love in which the ship rushes on with a fair wind behind it: *Frisch weht der Wind. . . .*

I cannot accept Mr Leavis's interpretation of the passage, 'I sat upon the shore/Fishing, with the arid plain behind me', as meaning that the poem 'exhibits no progression'. The comment upon what the thunder says would indicate, if other passages did not, that the poem does not 'end where it began'. It is true that the protagonist does not witness a revival of the waste land; but there are two important relationships involved in his case: a personal one as well as a general one. If secularization has destroyed, or is likely to destroy, modern civilization, the protagonist still has a private obligation to fulfil. Even if the civilization is breaking up—'London Bridge is falling down falling down falling down'—there remains the personal obligation: 'Shall I at least set my lands in order?' Consider in this connection the last sentences of Eliot's 'Thoughts After Lambeth': 'The World is trying the experiment of attempting to form a civilized but non-Christian mentality. The experiment will fail; but we must be very patient in awaiting its collapse; meanwhile redeeming the time: so that the Faith may be preserved alive through the dark ages before us; to renew and rebuild civilization, and save the World from suicide'.

The bundle of quotations with which the poem ends has a very definite relation to the general theme of the poem and to several of the major symbols used in the poem. Before Arnaut leaps back into the refining fire of Purgatory with joy he says: 'I am Arnaut who weep and go singing; contrite I see my past folly, and joyful I see before me the day I hope for. Now I pray you by that virtue which guides you to the summit of the stair, at times be mindful of my pain'. This note is carried forward by the quotation from *Pervigilium Veneris*: 'When shall I be like the swallow?' The allusion also connects with the Philomela symbol. (Eliot's note on the passage indicates this clearly.) The sister of Philomela was changed into a swallow as Philomela was changed into a nightingale. The protagonist is asking therefore when shall the spring, the time of love return, but also when will he be reborn out of his sufferings, and—with the special meaning which the symbol takes on from the preceding Dante quotation and from the earlier contexts already discussed—he is asking what is asked at the end of one of the minor poems: 'When will Time flow away?'

The quotation from 'El Desdichado', as Edmund Wilson has pointed out, indicates that the protagonist of the poem has been disinherited, robbed of his tradition. The ruined tower is perhaps also the Perilous Chapel, 'only the wind's home', and it is also the whole tradition in decay. The protagonist resolves to claim his tradition and rehabilitate it.

The quotation from *The Spanish Tragedy*—'Why then Ile fit

you. Hieronymo's mad againe'—is perhaps the most puzzling of all these quotations. It means, I believe, this: the protagonist's acceptance of what is in reality the deepest truth will seem to the present world mere madness. ('And still she cried, and still the world pursues,/"Jug Jug" to dirty ears'.) Hieronymo in the play, like Hamlet, was 'mad' for a purpose. The protagonist is conscious of the interpretation which will be placed on the words which follow—words which will seem to many apparently meaningless babble, but which contain the oldest and most permanent truth of the race:

Datta. Dayadhvam. Damyata.

After this statement comes the benediction:

Shantih Shantih Shantih

The foregoing account of *The Waste Land* is, of course, not to be substituted for the poem itself. Moreover, it certainly is not to be considered as representing *the method by which the poem was composed*. Much which the prose expositor must represent as though it had been consciously contrived, obviously was arrived at unconsciously and concretely.

The account given above is a statement merely of the 'prose meaning', and bears the same relation to the poem as does the 'prose meaning' of any other poem. But one need not perhaps apologize for setting forth such a statement explicitly, for *The Waste Land* has been almost consistently misinterpreted since its first publication. Even a critic so acute as Edmund Wilson has seen the poem as essentially a statement of despair and disillusionment, and this account sums up the stock interpretation of the poem. Indeed, the phrase, 'the poetry of drouth', has become a *cliché* of left-wing criticism. It is such a misrepresentation of *The Waste Land* as this which allows Eda Lou Walton to entitle an essay on contemporary poetry, 'Death in the Desert'; or which causes Waldo Frank to misconceive of Eliot's whole position and personality. But more than the meaning of one poem is at stake. If *The Waste Land* is not a world-weary cry of despair or a sighing after the vanished glories of the past, then not only the popular interpretation of the poem will have to be altered but also the general interpretations of post-war poetry which begin with such a misinterpretation as a premise.

Such misinterpretations involve also misconceptions of Eliot's technique. Eliot's basic method may be said to have passed relatively unnoticed. The popular view of the method used in *The Waste Land* may be described as follows: Eliot makes use of ironic contrasts between the glorious past and the sordid present—the crashing irony of

> But at my back from time to time I hear
> The sound of horns and motors, which shall bring
> Sweeney to Mrs Porter in the spring.

But this is to take the irony of the poem at the most superficial level, and to neglect the other dimensions in which it operates. And it is to neglect what are essentially more important aspects of his method. Moreover, it is to over-emphasize the difference between the method employed by Eliot in this poem and that employed by him in later poems.

The basic method used in *The Waste Land* may be described as the application of the principle of complexity. The poet works in terms of surface parallelisms which in reality make ironical contrasts, and in terms of surface contrasts which in reality constitute parallelisms. (The second group set up effects which may be described as the obverse of irony.) The two aspects taken together give the effect of chaotic experience ordered into a new whole though the realistic surface of experience is faithfully retained. The complexity of the experience is not violated by the apparent forcing upon it of a predetermined scheme.

The fortune-telling of 'The Burial of the Dead' will illustrate the general method very satisfactorily. On the surface of the poem the poet reproduces the patter of the charlatan, Madame Sosostris, and there is the surface irony: the contrast between the original use of the Tarot cards and the use made here. But each of the details (justified realistically in the palaver of the fortune-teller) assumes a new meaning in the general context of the poem. There is then in addition to the surface irony something of a Sophoclean irony too, and the 'fortune-telling' which is taken ironically by a twentieth-century audience becomes *true* as the poem develops—true in a sense in which Madame Sosostris herself does not think it true. The surface irony is thus reversed and becomes an irony on a deeper level. The items of her speech have only one reference in terms of the context of her speech: the 'man with three staves', the 'one-eyed merchant', the 'crowds of people, walking round in a ring', etc. But transferred to other contexts they become loaded with special meanings. To sum up, all the central symbols of the poem head up here, but here, in the only section in which they are explicitly bound together, the binding is slight and accidental. The deeper lines of association only emerge in terms of the total context as the poem develops—and this is, of course, exactly the effect which the poet intends.

This transference of items from an 'innocent' context into a context in which they become charged and transformed in meaning will account for many of the literary allusions in the poem. For example, the 'change of Philomel' is merely one of the items in the decorative detail in the room in the opening of 'A Game of Chess'. But the violent change of tense—'And still she cried, and still the world pursues'—makes it a comment upon, and a symbol of, the modern world. And further allusions to it through the course of the poem gradually equate it with the general theme of the poem. The allusions to *The Tempest* display the same method. The parallelism between Dante's Hell and the waste land of the Grail legends is fairly close; even the equation of Baudelaire's Paris to the waste land is fairly obvious. But the parallelism between the death by drowning in *The Tempest* and the death of the fertility god is, on the surface, merely accidental, and the first allusion to Ariel's song is merely an irrelevant and random association of the stream-of-consciousness:

> Is your card, the drowned Phœnician Sailor,
> (Those are pearls that were his eyes. Look!)

And on its second appearance in 'A Game of Chess' it is still only an item in the protagonist's abstracted reverie. Even the association of *The Tempest* symbol with the Grail legends in the lines

> While I was fishing in the dull canal
>
> .   .   .   .   .
>
> Musing upon the king my brother's wreck.

and in the passage which follows, is ironical merely. But the associations have been established, even though they may seem to be made in ironic mockery, and when we come to the passage, 'Death by Water', with its change of tone, they assert themselves positively. We have a sense of revelation out of material apparently accidentally thrown together. I have called the effect the obverse of irony, for the method like that of irony, is indirect, though the effect is positive rather than negative.

The 'melting' of the characters into each other is, of course, an aspect of this general process. Elizabeth and the girl born at Highbury both ride on the Thames, one in the barge of state, the other supine in a narrow canoe, and they are both Thames-nymphs, who are violated and thus are like the Rhine-nymphs who have also been violated, etc. With the characters as with the other symbols, the surface relationships may be accidental and apparently trivial and they may be made either ironically or through random association or in hallucination, but in the total context of the poem the deeper relationships are revealed. The effect is a sense of the oneness of experience, and of the unity of all periods, and with this, a sense that the general theme of the poem is true. But the theme has not been imposed—it has been revealed.

This complication of parallelisms and contrasts makes, of course, for ambiguity, but the ambiguity, in part, resides in the poet's fidelity to the complexity of experience. The symbols resist complete equation with a simple meaning. To take an example, 'rock' throughout the poem seems to be one of the 'desert' symbols. For example, the 'dry stone' gives 'no sound of water'; woman in the waste land is 'the Lady of the Rocks', and most pointed of all, there is the long delirium passage in 'What the Thunder Said': 'Here is no water but only rock', etc. So much for its general meaning, but in 'The Burial of the Dead' occur the lines

> *Only*
> *There is shadow under this red rock,*
> *(Come in under the shadow of this red rock).*

Rock here is a place of refuge. (Moreover, there may also be a reference to the Grail symbolism. In *Parzival*, the Grail is a stone: 'And this stone all men call the grail. . . . As children the Grail doth call them, 'neath its shadow they wax and grow'.) The paradox, life through death, penetrates the symbol itself.

To take an even clearer case of this paradoxical use of symbols, consider the lines which occur in the hyacinth-girl passage. The vision gives obviously a sense of the richness and beauty of life. It is a moment of ecstasy (the basic imagery is obviously sexual); but the moment in its intensity is like death. The protagonist looks in that moment into the 'heart of light, the silence', and so looks into—not richness—but blankness: he is neither 'living nor dead'. The symbol of life stands also for a kind of death. This duality of function may, of course, extend to a whole passage. For example, consider:

> Where fishmen lounge at noon: where the walls
> Of Magnus Martyr hold
> Inexplicable splendour of Ionian white and gold.

The function of the passage is to indicate the poverty into which religion has fallen: the splendid church now surrounded by the poorer districts. But the passage has an opposed effect also: the fishmen in the 'public bar in Lower Thames Street' next to the church have a meaningful life which has been largely lost to the secularized upper and middle classes.

The poem would undoubtedly be 'clearer' if every symbol had one, unequivocal, meaning; but the poem would be thinner, and less honest. For the poet has not been content to develop a didactic allegory in which the symbols are two-dimensional items adding up directly to the sum of the general scheme. They represent dramatized instances of the theme, embodying in their own nature the fundamental paradox of the theme.

We shall better understand why the form of the poem is right and inevitable if we compare Eliot's theme to Dante's and to Spenser's. Eliot's theme is not the statement of a faith held and agreed upon (Dante's *Divine Comedy*) nor is it the projection of a 'new' system of beliefs (Spenser's *Færie Queene*). Eliot's theme is the rehabilitation of a system of beliefs, known but now discredited. Dante did not have to 'prove' his statement; he could assume it and move within it about a poet's business. Eliot does not care, like Spenser, to force the didacticism. He prefers to stick to the poet's business. But, unlike Dante, he cannot assume acceptance of the statement. A direct approach is calculated to elicit powerful 'stock responses' which will prevent the poem's being *read* at all. Consequently, the only method is to work by indirection. The 'Christian' material is at the centre, but the poet never deals with it directly. The theme of resurrection is made on the surface in terms of the fertility rites; the words which the thunder speaks are Sanskrit words.

Cleanth Brooks

We have been speaking as if the poet were a strategist trying to win acceptance from a hostile audience. But of course this is true only in a sense. The poet himself is audience as well as speaker; we state the problem more exactly if we state it in terms of the poet's integrity rather than in terms of his strategy. He is so much a man of his own age that he can indicate his attitude toward the Christian tradition without falsity only in terms of the difficulties of a rehabilitation; and he is so much a poet and so little a propagandist that he can be sincere only as he presents his theme concretely and dramatically.

To put the matter in still other terms: the Christian terminology is for the poet here a mass of *clichés*. However 'true' he may feel the terms to be, he is still sensitive to the fact that they operate superficially as *clichés*, and his method of necessity must be a process of bringing them to life again. The method adopted in *The Waste Land* is thus violent and radical, but thoroughly necessary. For the renewing and vitalizing of symbols which have been crusted over with a distorting familiarity demands the type of organization which we have already commented on in discussing particular passages: the statement of surface similarities which are ironically revealed to be dissimilarities, and the association of apparently obvious dissimilarities which culminates in a later realization that the dissimilarities are only superficial—that the chains of likeness are in reality fundamental. In this way the statement of beliefs emerges *through* confusion and cynicism—not in spite of them.

Ash Wednesday

THE INSISTENCE throughout is upon states of feeling. What Eliot says of Dante's *Paradiso* is also true of his own poem *Ash Wednesday*. It is religious poetry which is not didactic in any degree: it does not explain the doctrine or discipline of his faith, but it communicates something of what is felt in apprehending and undergoing them. The poem may be illustrated by generalizations about religious experience but it contains none: it is, so to speak, the thing itself.

There is great variety of rhythmical effects—even Yeats, who is far from doing justice to Eliot's poetry, allows that there is rhythmical animation in *Ash Wednesday*; but the particular characteristics of its music are delicacy and purity.

Ash Wednesday is impersonal and objective in a sense in which, for instance, the best poems of George Herbert are not. The 'I' who speaks is not so much a personality as a will. And in keeping with this impersonality, at its peaks and climaxes the poetry passes into the anonymous language of the Church: 'Pray for us now and at the hour of our death'; 'Speak the word only'; 'After this our exile'; 'Suffer me not to be separated'; 'And let my cry come unto Thee'.

It is evident that although in *Ash Wednesday* Eliot follows Dante in many respects, he does not limit the suggestions of his symbols as Dante does, or as his commentators have done for him. Nor does he present the reader with a narrative which embodies his 'states of feeling'. Nevertheless with some good will, and using the order of Dante's experiences as a guide, it is possible to disengage a 'story' from the poem. The sequence begins with a poem of which the centre is the renunciation of a 'blessèd face' and voice: this is followed by a vision of spiritual renewal, presided over by a Beatrice-figure who is also the Church, as Beatrice was also Theology; then there comes the ascent of a spiritual stair, with a backward glance at carnal loveliness: and then a scene in a garden or churchyard where 'she' reappears, transfigured and glorified. One feels, however, that if the poet had attached much importance to the narrative element he would have made it more prominent. The stress is perhaps rather on the sequence of images: there is, as he remarks in his preface to the translation of St-J. Perse's *Anabase* which was published in the same year as *Ash Wednesday*, 'a logic of the imagination as well as a logic of concepts': and *Ash Wednesday* relies as much on one as on the other.

The language of the poem achieves that 'easy commerce of the old and new' which is spoken of in *Little Gidding*. In the fourth poem, for instance, between two lines which might almost be translations of Dante, there is a line which could only be modern:

> *Going in white and blue, in Mary's colour,*
> *Talking of trivial things*
> *In ignorance and in knowledge of eternal dolour.*

An element of contrast is intended: but it is not sharp: there is congruity too. The images which are traditional—the desert, the bones, the rose, the unicorn, combine in the same 'easy commerce' with the white sails, the 'lilac and brown hair', the bent golden-rod, the wind in the yew-trees: there is no disharmony between the agèd eagle, which is traditional, and the agèd shark, which is an invented symbol.

The six parts of the poem are connected by recurrent phrases and images: 'Because I do not hope'; 'The deceitful face of hope and of despair'; 'Although I do not hope'; 'Because these wings are no longer wings to fly'; 'Unbroken wings'. The silent sister between the yew-trees is present in each of the last three poems: in the last two the imagery of the desert and the garden modulates into that of the rocks and the sea.

I

The first poem of *Ash Wednesday* begins with a line which is an almost literal translation of the first line of a poem of Cavalcanti's: 'Because I do not hope to turn again'. It is evidently not essential to make the connection with Cavalcanti: but the reader who does will find that it reinforces some of the suggestions of the English poem. Cavalcanti's adoration of the ideal figure of the Lady is part of the 'organization of sensibility' which is adopted in *Ash Wednesday*, and in this poem, written when he was dying in exile, his worship of the Lady is the only positive feeling, all else being exhaustion and despair. The line from Shakespeare's sonnet, 'Desiring this man's art and that man's scope' (Eliot has altered *art* to *gift*) is bound for most readers to carry some of its context with it:

> When, in disgrace with fortune and men's eyes,
> I all alone beweep my outcast state
> And trouble deaf heaven with my bootless cries,
> And look upon myself and curse my fate:
> Wishing me like to one more rich in hope. . . .

The themes of introspection, solitariness and despair are found in both poems quoted: and both are relevant to the first poem of *Ash Wednesday*, though the lines incorporated into Eliot's verse have so much taken on the colour of his own that they do not strike primarily as allusions. 'Mature poets steal'; the remark is well illustrated here.

The title under which the six poems now stand prepares us for poetry concerned mainly with the penitential side of the spiritual life: and the first poem deals with the processes of self-exploration and self-examination with which that begins. The movement of the first three stanzas is slow and grave. The repetition of 'because' gives the impression of 'la raison raisonnant'; the intellect is establishing the relations of things. 'Strive to strive' and 'know I shall not know' suggest the piercing through layer on layer of motive. 'I do not hope' is reiterated. In his preface to a translation of Pascal's *Pensées* Eliot speaks of a despair which was 'a necessary prelude to, and element in, the joy of faith'. This surely might be an account of the despair which is present in the first two verses of this poem.

The 'turn' in the first line establishes the pivot on which the whole work is to hang: in all those parts of the poem which deal with the labours of the reason and the will the turning movement is to recur. It is not to be defined as a turn from unrighteousness to righteousness, from the world to God, or from past to present: it is sometimes one and sometimes the other, and the ambiguity is fundamental. It is by the 'turn' that the two worlds between which the poem moves are kept present to our minds. *Ash Wednesday* is a poem full of connections which are too subtle for the intellect, a poem which continually 'teases us out of thought'; but one need not go into it deeply in order to discover that the poem is full of suggestions of reverses and circlings, that in the whole there may be discerned a kind of spiral movement. There is a sermon of Lancelot Andrewes on the opening words of the Epistle for Ash Wednesday 'Turn ye even unto me, saith the Lord. . . .' which it is interesting to compare in this respect: 'Now at this time is the turning of the year. . . . Everything now turning that we also would make it our time to turn to God in. . . . Upon this turning, *cardo vertitur*, the hinge turns, of our well or evil doing for ever. . . . Repentance itself is nothing but a kind of circling. . . . Which circle consists of two turnings. . . . First a turn wherein we look forward to God and with our whole heart resolve to turn to Him. Then a turn again wherein we look backward to our sins wherein we have turned from God. . . . The wheel turns apace, and if we turn not the rather these turnings may overtake us'.

The 'agèd eagle' in the first verse is a striking image: it has been complained of by one distinguished critic as a solemn and self-pitying description of a poet then in his early forties. Allen Tate and others have pointed out the irony of the expression and it can hardly be doubted that they are right. It is a mocking piece of self-characterization, a poet's ironic attack on the grandiose conceptions which poets sometimes entertain of themselves. The line from Shakespeare has already suggested that in this passage Eliot is concerned with poetic activity. Nothing could be more unlike Eliot than to call himself in all seriousness an agèd eagle, meaning thereby to suggest the grandeur and pathos of the poet's calling. In his essay on Baudelaire, which is contemporary with *Ash Wednesday*, Eliot mentions Baudelaire's poem *L'Albatros*.

> Le Poète est semblable au prince des nuées
> Qui hante la tempête et se rit de l'archer.
> Exilé sur le sol, au milieu des huées
> Ses ailes de géant l'empêchent de marcher.

'*Ses ailes de géant*' Eliot cites as an example of the 'romantic detritus' amongst Baudelaire's imagery. The poet as an agèd eagle, intended seriously, would surely fall under the same condemnation.

But there is another sense in which the agèd eagle may be taken. Allen Tate describes it as a secular image, but it is usually very much the opposite. Since the Psalmist wrote 'Thy youth shall be renewed as the eagle's' the image has been constantly used in religious contexts as one of spiritual regeneration; for the Middle Ages the rejuvenation of the agèd eagle was the symbol of Baptismal grace.[1] 'Why should the agèd eagle stretch his wings', although it primarily suggests a mocking statement of the apparent failure of poetic vigour, may well suggest also a reluctance to embark on the exacting process of spiritual rebirth. In this sense it is another instance of the stress on the pain of rebirth which haunts Eliot's poetry from 'April is the cruellest month' of *The Waste Land* to 'I've been born and once is enough' (*Sweeney Agonistes*) and 'This birth was hard and bitter agony' (*Journey of the Magi*).

It has often been said that the stress in Eliot's religious poetry is on the cost of the spiritual life. D. W. Harding says that 'the renunciation is more vividly communicated than the advance for which it is made'. I should not say that this is true of *Ash Wednesday*, however just it may be as applied to *A Song for Simeon* or *The Journey of the Magi*. The outstanding effect of *Ash Wednesday* is one of movement—'the detail of the pattern is movement'— of progress and growth: precarious—'wavering between the profit and the loss' even in the last poem of the six—but still strong and living.

That there is a conflict is, of course, admitted: it is evident in the contradictory elements of

> *The infirm glory of the positive hour*

and

> *The one veritable transitory power.*

[1] A note on Dante's dream of the Eagle (*Purg.* ix) in the Temple Classics edition reminds one that in the Medieval Bestiaries the eagle is said to fly up in his old age into the circle of fire, where he burns off all his feathers and falls blinded into a fountain of water whence he issues with his youth renewed. Cf. *The Family Reunion*:

> And what of the terrified spirit
> Compelled to be reborn
> To rise toward the violent sun
> Wet wings into the rain cloud. . . .

A quotation from Eliot's remarks on Baudelaire is perhaps relevant here. 'Either because he cannot adjust himself to the actual world he has to reject it in favour of Heaven or Hell: or because he has the perception of Heaven and Hell he rejects the present world: both ways of putting it are tenable'. The first stanza of *Ash Wednesday* suggests the first hypothesis: the second stanza suggests the other. The last clause of the Lord's Prayer seems to be in the background of these verses: 'thine is the kingdom, the power, and the glory, for ever and ever': it is against this that the 'usual reign', the 'infirm glory' and the 'transitory power' are measured and seem to fall short.

> *Because I cannot drink*
> *There, where trees flower, and springs flow, for*
> *there is nothing again.*

The mirage recedes: the reality of which 'human kind cannot bear very much' prevails in the positive statements of the third stanza:

> *Because I know that time is always time*
> *And place is always and only place*
> *And what is actual is actual only for one time*
> *And only for one place.*

The 'I' is clearing away the processes of self-deception by which the actual conditions of human life are masked: the first step is the admission that 'time is always time'. The mind is now, to use a phrase from *Murder in the Cathedral*, 'whole in the present'. The rhythm, which has been halting except in lines which recall the unattainable, quickens and becomes resolute.

> *I rejoice that things are as they are and*
> *I renounce the blessed face*
> *And renounce the voice.*

The will comes into prominence in the joyful acceptance of things as they are. That it is a *blessèd* face which is renounced is at first surprising. A Dante-Beatrice relationship is suggested in much of *Ash Wednesday*: and Dante's apprehension of God was *through* Beatrice. But Dante's 'first light' had to end with Beatrice's death and the renunciation here may be of the physical presence of a beloved woman. Or possibly it may be that courtesy of the spirit which accepts the absence of spiritual consolations without complaint, and is content to wait in stillness.

Ash Wednesday

In the next line the stress falls naturally on the word *cannot*: 'Because I cannot hope to turn again'. It is as if the conflict is ended, one party having sustained defeat.

> Consequently I rejoice, having to construct something
> Upon which to rejoice.

The paradox is evident. The poem itself may well be the construction 'upon which to rejoice'.

The poetry of *Ash Wednesday* has been described as solitary, and so much of it is, as might be expected from the title. But the poem is not solitary throughout: it alternates between solitude and the consciousness of the body of the Church, with the alternation expressed in two lines of *The Rock*:

> Let us mourn in a private chamber, learning the way of penitence,
> And then let us learn the joyful communion of saints.

From the beginning of the fourth stanza onwards there are shifts to the plural: the 'I' remembers that it is one of many. In the last two stanzas the poem approaches the verge of prayer: the need for mercy is recognized, and judgment deprecated: there is an effort to dismiss the recollection of the past and to quiet the activity of the mind. The tone is grave and there is complete simplicity. In the last verse the wings which are

> no longer wings to fly
> But merely vans to beat the air

are in one sense suggestive of impotence and melancholy: as if the self sees that from the point of view of the natural man it is decayed from its original vigour: but 'vans beating the air' may also suggest the winnowing movement which separates corn from chaff. The wings are serving a purpose, making the air thoroughly small and dry, so that the will, the instrument of prayer, may take over. There is focusing of attention,

> Teach us to care and not to care

and the long stream of meditation comes to an end in the stillness of prayer.

The language of the last two lines is no longer the poet's own: the 'I' is lost in the voice of the Church invoking Mary. The repetition of 'now and at the hour of our death' stresses the

43

relation of the present to eternity. Life is felt as

The time of tension between birth and dying

in the first poem as well as in the sixth.

II

It seems that the second poem of *Ash Wednesday*, originally *Salutation I*, was the first in order of composition. In its original form an epigraph *e voi significando* related it to a passage in the *Purgatorio* in which Bonagiunta da Lucca, a poet of the older fashion, recognizes in Dante the new poet of the sweet new style. 'I am one who when love inspires find melody and as he dictates to my mind, so do I give utterance'. Of the six poems which make up *Ash Wednesday* this is the one which most strikingly shows Eliot's *stil nuovo*. It is unlike anything that he had written before and perhaps unlike anything else that has been written in English, in its cadences and in its suggestions. Beneath the clarity and animation of its surface are themes which are the staple of Catholic Christianity: the renewing power of grace, the vicarious life of the Church, the doctrine of the Communion of Saints. The form is definite, objective and impersonal. The poem might well be an expression of that 'higher dream' whose disappearance Eliot regrets in his book on Dante. It has pre-eminently the air of something 'given': there is a miraculous ease and lightness about the rhythms and about the experience which they communicate. In itself a complete and rounded poem, in relation to the other parts of the sequence this vision is one of the 'hints and guesses, hints followed by guesses' which are spoken of in *The Dry Salvages*. The first poem showed the struggles of the individual and the labours of the reason and the will: in the second grace is at work and everything is easy.

As I am forgotten
And would be forgotten, so I would forget
Thus devoted, concentrated in purpose.

There is no wavering between the profit and the loss here:

We are glad to be scattered, we did little good to each other.

The subject of the vision is death: not the death of the body but a spiritual dissolution, a dying to self, which from the

spiritual point of view (and here no other is relevant) is seen as
wholly gain. It is evident that the elements of the dream come
partly from Dante and partly from the Scriptures, in particular
from the later chapters of *Ezekiel*. Throughout the sequence
Eliot adopts Dante's 'organization of sensibility—the contrast
between higher and lower carnal love, the transition from
Beatrice living to Beatrice dead, rising to the cult of the Virgin'.
The Lady who is saluted is a figure who in relation to the 'I'
of the poem is something of what Lucia, Matelda and, supremely,
Beatrice are to the Dante of the *Purgatorio*, a Lady who 'helps
him on his way': it is

> Because of the goodness of this Lady
> And because of her loveliness and because
> She honours the Virgin in meditation

that the bones 'shine with brightness'. The 'Because . . . and
because' echo the 'Because I do not hope' of the first poem, but
a different logic obtains here. And as what Beatrice is for Dante,
Mary is, in a sense, for all; so that at a given point in the *Purgatorio* critics are not sure whether it is Mary or Beatrice who is
spoken of: either may be 'the lady who above, acquires grace
for us'; so the Lady who 'is withdrawn in a white gown, to
contemplation', the 'Lady of Silences', is invoked in lines which
recall some of the Virgin's titles.

Dante's spotted leopard is a gay but sinister beast: the three
white leopards here are, on the contrary, agents of good, and
Matthiessen is surely right in rejecting the suggestion that they
personify the World, the Flesh and the Devil. They are more
likely to be the goodness of the Lady, her loveliness, and the
fact that she honours the Virgin in meditation.

The whiteness and the brightness of the bones are lovely. The
dissembling of the 'I' is not conceived of as an outrage: whatever
may be the similarities of technique the mood of the scene is in
complete contrast to that evoked by the destruction of the body
in Baudelaire's *Voyage au Cythére*. The gruesomeness of some of
the details—'my legs my heart my liver and that which had been
contained in the hollow round of my skull' and 'the indigestible
portions which the leopards reject'—is nearer to being playful
than horrific. One may find in this part of the poem something
of that 'alliance of levity and seriousness, by which the serious-

ness is intensified', of that 'toughness which may be confused with cynicism by the tender-minded', which Eliot attributes to Marvell. There is no hint of pathos. The 'I' co-operates in the work of dissolution:

> *I who am here dissembled*
> *Proffer my deeds to oblivion, and my love*
> *To the posterity of the desert and the fruits of the gourd.*

There is enough of him left to see and record the scene—

> *It is this which recovers*
> *My guts, the strings of my eyes and the indigestible portions*
> *Which the leopards reject.*

Perhaps this is a hint that there must always be a residuum of self in a poet, without which there would be no need to write poetry. It is not necessary to account for the setting by a quotation from St John of the Cross, 'an immense desert . . . the more delectable, pleasant and lovely for its secrecy, vastness and solitude', although this may be relevant to the spiritual state which is being described. It is certainly a 'delectable' desert, without heat or thirst: the sand is a 'blessing', the day 'cool'. The paradox of the garden in the desert and the rose in the desert are to be found in *Isaiah*. The juniper-tree recalls that under which Elijah despaired: 'he requested for himself that he might die. And as he lay and slept under the juniper-tree, behold, then an angel touched him and said unto him, "Arise and eat".' The bones in the desert and the prophesying to the wind come from Ezekiel's vision of the regeneration of Israel—a passage connected in the liturgy with the spiritual regeneration of baptism. 'Our bones are dried and our hope is lost.'

It is a kind of litany, not of supplication but of rejoicing, which the bones sing, 'chirping' to the Lady of Silences 'with the burden of the grasshopper'. The phrase here surely has none of the melancholy associations of its original context, in *Ecclesiastes*; there is faintness perhaps and feebleness, but it is difficult for 'chirping' to have anything but a cheerful sound. As has been said the 'Lady of Silences' at first suggests the Lady who is engaged in contemplation: but the paradoxical attributes in the subsequent lines suggest a more transcendent figure, the Virgin herself or the Church. *Rosa Mystica* is one of Mary's titles. In the *Paradiso* she is that 'Rose in which the Word

Divine made itself flesh'. 'Terminate torment of love unsatisfied' and 'End of the endless journey to no end' seem to derive from St Bernard's hymn to the Virgin in *Paradiso* XXX in which she is called 'Termine fisso d'eterno consiglio'. But the Rose of Sharon is a title given to Christ Himself, and Dante sees the whole of the saints in Paradise, the Church triumphant, as the petals of one white rose. In the earlier version 'The single Rose' was followed by a line now omitted: 'With worm-eaten petals', which would suggest the inroads of evil on the Church militant.[2] But the line may well have been left out of the later version because it limited the suggestions of the Rose.

In the earlier version the lines

> Rose of Memory
> Rose of Forgetfulness

were echoed by two other lines, now deleted, after the phrase 'Grace to the Mother':

> For the end of remembering
> End of forgetting. . . .

The stress on memory and forgetfulness, both conceived as benefits, recalls the streams of Lethe and Eunoe which run through Dante's Earthly Paradise or Garden of Eden. 'On this side it (the water) descends with a virtue which takes from men the memory of sin: on the other it restores the memory of every good deed'. In the first part of *Ash Wednesday* the poet prays that he may forget

> These matters that with myself I too much discuss
> Too much explain.

In the second the prayer is answered.

The paradox of 'the Garden where all loves end' and of 'the Garden where all love ends' is not to be limited to one interpretation: but the obvious sense is that while the lower loves come to an end here, in the sense of being concluded, the

[2]Cf. George Herbert's poem *Church-Rents and Schisms*:

> Brave rose (alas!) where art thou? in the chair
> Where thou didst lately so triumph and shine
> A worm doth sit, whose many feet and hair
> Are the more foul, the more thou wert divine.
> This, this hath done it, this did bite the root
> And bottom of the leaves. . . .

higher love here reaches its destination, its consummation.

After the Litany the poem returns to the firm, light, dancing rhythms of the opening:

> Under a juniper-tree the bones sang, scattered and shining
> We are glad to be scattered, we did little good to each other.

The bones seem no longer to represent a single person, but many having undergone the same transmutation,

> Forgetting themselves and each other, united
> In the quiet of the desert.

Personalities are sunk in the communion of saints, intent on a common object of worship; that is not the whole meaning of the passage but it is perhaps part of it.

The concluding lines of the poem quote Ezekiel's description of the dividing of the land, which occurs after the vision of the building of the Temple and the healing of the waters: 'This is the land which ye shall divide by lot unto the tribes of Israel for inheritance: and these are their portions, saith the Lord God.'

> This is the land which ye
> Shall divide by lot. And neither division nor unity
> Matters. This is the land. We have our inheritance.

The bones are as little careful of their own rights or envious of those of others as the blessed in Dante's *Paradiso*. The second poem ends on a note of absolute assurance and content.

III

The vision of the desert and the Lady is over: it may have helped the 'I' of the poem on his way as the first of Dante's three dreams advanced him to the entrance of Purgatory: but, the dream ended, Dante has to climb the steps into Purgatory unaided, and the third poem of *Ash Wednesday* returns, as the opening lines suggest, to the labours of the will. The struggle is resumed: the 'I' who did not hope to turn, turns again and again as he mounts the stair: the struggle is now with the evil whose presence is felt in the 'devil of the stairs' and the 'fetid air'. Evil is represented here, as it is in *Murder in the Cathedral*, by images repugnant to sense and touch. Eliot's stair is his own version of the usual image of spiritual progress: it is not pure symbol; it exists in its own right, too, with its banister, its damp, dark step, its window on to the meadow.

The title of this part when published separately was *'al som de l'escalina'*, a phrase from the Provençal speech of Arnaut's to which Eliot refers so often: 'Now I pray you, by that Goodness which guideth you to the summit of the stairway, be mindful in due time of my pain.' It has been suggested by several critics that the three stairs of *Ash Wednesday* correspond to the three stages of Dante's Purgatorial Mount. This is evidently not to be pressed. It seems possible that the recollection of these has mingled with that of the three steps into purgatory, of which the surfaces are symbolic. 'There where we came, at the first step was white marble, so polished and smooth that it mirrored me therein as I appear. The second darker was than perse, of a stone ragged and calcined, cracked in its length and in its breadth: the third seemed to me of porphyry, so flaming red as blood that spurts from a vein.' Dante's commentators explain these as sincerity, contrition and love: or contrition, confession and expiation by the blood of Christ. The devil with the deceitful face may owe something to the image mirrored in the first step and the damp jagged stair might well be his version of that

tinto più che perso
d'una petrina ruvida ed arsiccia
crepata per lo lungo e per traverso

by which Dante represents the soul's realization of its own evil. In the image of the old man's mouth and the shark's gullet the 'I' sees its own malice, the malice of the 'old man' in the Pauline sense, old because unregenerate. The peculiar repulsiveness of the rotten tooth is used in a similar way in *The Waste Land*: 'Dead mountain mouth of carious teeth that cannot spit': and in the later poetry the tooth or fang is often used as suggestive of malice.

The springtime scene perceived through the voluptuously shaped window of the third stair is lovely, but with a nostalgic loveliness, enchanting and relaxing, which is in complete contrast to that of the life-giving, paradisal spring of the next poem. The scene and the music are not sinister in themselves, but they distract the mind from the ascent of the staircase. In *Murder in the Cathedral* imagery which has some resemblance to that of the 'pasture scene' is used to represent the 'natural vigour in the venial sin'. The first and least formidable of the tempters reminds the Archbishop of 'Fluting in the meadows': and Thomas remembers, 'Not worth forgetting'.

The third stair itself is not described. The ascent of it is not achieved unaided and its climax is a movement of humility. The words of the centurion are associated by the Church with the rite of Holy Communion and it is perhaps that which is *Ash Wednesday's* equivalent of the Purgatorial healing, or the step of red porphyry. 'Speak the word only and thy servant shall be healed.'

IV

The fourth poem returns to the 'higher dream'. There is much of Dante here. The 'eternal dolour' and the appeal of Arnaut recall Dante verbally, and the whole scene is related to that in which Dante meets a Beatrice 'risen from flesh to spirit', in the Earthly Paradise. The scene is precise in detail but vague in outline: 'who walked' may refer to a single figure or to several, according to the interpretation given to 'Who moved among the others as they walked': the one who wears white light may or may not be the same as the 'silent sister'. The first lines

> Who walked between the violet and the violet
> Who walked between
> The various ranks of varied green

may suggest a figure threading its way through the paths of a garden: but the violet and the green are not committed to being flowers or leaves: they may be taken as liturgical colours, or as formal order, or carefulness, discipline, 'concentration of purpose'. The colours used in this poem are all capable of symbolical meanings: the violet of penance, the green of hope, the white of purity, the blue of celestial things; but it is 'blue of larkspur' as well as 'of Mary's colour'. Surface appearances here are not merely to be transcended, although of course they suggest meanings which transcend them. Thus 'larkspur' too may have ethereal suggestions as in Hopkins' poems on St Dorothea.

The nunlike figure through whom the scene is evoked is not described: the stages of her progress are stressed—she 'moved among the others', 'talking of trivial things', before she 'made strong the fountains'—a renewing of the sources of life for others which recalls the activity of contemplation to which the Lady of the second poem withdrew. There is a contrast between the simplicity and ordinariness of her behaviour, and her achievement in the spiritual realm: between her ignorance and her knowledge. 'Eternal dolour' at first suggests the pains of Hell,

Per me si va nell' eterno dolore,

but the dolour may be that of the Passion. There is no 'I' in this poem: but the 'sovegna vos' of Arnaut relates the figure in white and blue to a penitent who asks for her prayers.

It was in the Divine Pageant that Dante saw the glorified Beatrice and felt the tokens of the ancient flame. After a break in this poem the years move in a sort of procession,

bearing
Away the fiddles and the flutes, restoring
One who moves in the time between sleep and waking, wearing
White light folded, sheathed about her.

The 'white light' and the 'bright cloud of tears' are Eliot's version of that 'imagery of light' by which, as he says, Dante conveys the notion of beatitude. Dante several times describes figures swathed (*fasciato*) in light or joy, and *swathed* has perhaps suggested both the purely pictorial *folded* and the *sheathed* which adds suggestions of the flower and the sword. It is not only the figure of a lost love which is given back:

The new years walk, restoring
With a new verse the ancient rhyme.

The poetic power which in the first poem seemed to be felt as declining is rejuvenated. 'Restoring the years' modulates into 'Redeeming the time', the urgent cry that echoes through *Burnt Norton*:

Redeem
The unread vision in the higher dream
While jewelled unicorns draw by the gilded hearse.

The mysterious effect is surely intended: it is perhaps part of the 'unread vision'. The unicorn is in place in the medieval and formal setting of this poem (one finds it, for instance, in Cavalcanti), and the whole line continues the effect of the procession or pageant, conjuring up a picture like those Florentine engravings which illustrate Petrarch's Triumphs. It is in the Triumph of Chastity that the car drawn by unicorns appears: what is suggested here is rather the apparent Triumph of Time.

The figure in white and blue who 'talked of trivial things' is now the 'silent sister'. The garden god is here too, but his flute is 'breathless', impotent to enchant and distract. It is the silence of the sister which is powerful and when she 'signs', perhaps making the sign of the Cross, the garden springs into fresh life. The yews which frame the nun-like figure are symbols which occur several times in Eliot's poetry from *Animula* onwards— 'Pray for Floret by the boar-hound slain between the yew-trees'. If they have a literary ancestry I am ignorant of it. But the yews' suggestions of mortality and immortality are not recondite. As the churchyard tree the yew must first suggest death: but it perhaps is the churchyard tree because its long life symbolizes immortality, and because it is, in Sir Thomas Browne's phrase 'an embleme of Resurrection from its perpetual verdure'.

The wind that is to 'shake a thousand whispers from the yew' must in the context suggest the spirit of God, as in the Canticles: 'Blow upon my garden that the spices thereof may flow out.' The line suggests a 'divine event'. But it is also merely the wind in the yew trees, with its own unfathomable meaning. There is a line in *Anabase* which has something of the same sense of expectancy: 'I foretell you the time of a great blessing and the felicity of leaves in our dreams.'[3]

The dream-scene makes death enviable and life an exile, as they appear in the *Salve Regina*, the invocation of Mary as Queen. It is with a phrase from this prayer that the poem ends: 'And after this our exile show unto us the blessed fruit of thy womb, Jesus.' On this undertone the poem moves to the mystery of the Logos.

[3]Mr Raymond Preston in *Four Quartets Rehearsed* (Sheed & Ward, 1946) indicates an allusion in *Ash Wednesday* to the bird in Grimm's fairy tale ' The Juniper Tree.' The tree in the poem is perhaps also to be connected with that in the fairy tale. When Marlinchen buried the little boy's bones beneath it the juniper ' began to stir itself—just as if someone was rejoicing and clapping his hands.' Marlinchen goes away ' as gay and happy as if her brother were still alive.'

Ash Wednesday

V

In the fifth poem the scene widens from the intense experience of an individual soul, with its circlings between past and present, God and self, to the world whirling 'about the centre of the silent Word'. The 'I' who speaks here is not the worshipper but the Deity, using the Reproaches, the liturgical expression of Christ's griefs. 'O my people, what have I done unto thee, or wherein have I wearied thee? Testify against me. Because I brought thee forth from the land of Egypt thou hast prepared a cross for thy Saviour.' This poem is to *Ash Wednesday* something of what *The Sacrifice* is to Herbert's Temple: the other poems in the Temple, with few exceptions, deal with the soul's efforts to attain to God; in *The Sacrifice* the situation is reversed and Herbert, rehearsing the events of the Passion, shows Christ appealing to man:

> *O all ye who pass by, whose eye and mind*
> *To worldly things are sharp, but to me blind:*
> *To me who took eyes that I might you find*
> *Was ever grief like Mine?*

The rhythms with which the fifth poem opens are decided, intricate, almost declamatory, after the delicate and tentative music of Part IV: the first stanza leaves an impression of extreme mental activity and stress, which is something like the effect of Andrewes' sermons, from which a phrase is borrowed. The play on 'word' and 'world' has caused the passage to remind one critic of Gertrude Stein's prose: but much of it is already present in the English version of the first chapter of St John's Gospel, the hymn to the Logos, on which the verse is based.

The Incarnation and the Passion are brought together: the silence of the Word is that of the speechless Babe and of the Christ who before his accusers 'opened not his mouth'. Silence as the condition of spiritual events has been stressed throughout *Ash Wednesday*: and many hints are now fulfilled—the 'speech without word and Word of no speech' of Part II; 'Speak the word only' of Part III; 'Spoke no word' of Part IV:

> *Still is the unspoken word the Word unheard,*
> *The Word without a word, the Word within*
> *The world and for the world.*

53

The second stanza explores the whole world for the right response to the Word.

> *No place of grace for those who avoid the face*
> *No time to rejoice for those who walk among noise and deny the voice.*

The face and the voice which were renounced in the first poem are here avoided and denied. The distinction is clear: to renounce is to refuse to make a claim; to avoid or deny is to refuse a claim that is made.

In the third and fourth verses there is a more personal note: the poet turns from surveying the world as a spectator to including himself in the number of those who, though they have responded, have not responded fully: and the rhythm becomes slower and quieter, lingering on the rhymes of the last line:

> *Pray for those who chose and oppose.*

The conflict is not only that which springs from the unresolvable tension between the material and the spiritual. The line

> *torn on the horn between season and season . . . power and power*

suggests also the strain imposed on those who are 'conscious, without remission, of a Christian and non-Christian alternative at moments of choice' (*Idea of a Christian Society*). The last verse enacts the struggle of man dealing with his own cowardice, conscious of the disparity between the outward allegiance and the inner betrayal. The imagery of the rocks and the desert presents a sequence of strenuous spiritual effort which seems to end in victory: 'Spitting from the mouth the withered apple-seed' may suggest the act of confession, the opening formula of which is quoted in the next poem: 'Bless me father, for I have sinned'. It may also, with a wider bearing, suggest that 'diminution of the traces of original sin' which Baudelaire saw as the essence of true civilization.

VI

The last poem in many ways summons up the first. But the 'I' is not merely back at the point from which he started: it is now 'Although I do not hope' instead of 'Because'. While in the first poem the emphasis was on not hoping, not striving, here in spite of the assertions that life is a 'brief transit', 'a dreamcrossed twilight', there are aspirations after natural vigour and unfettered movement: not

> *Why should the aged eagle stretch its wings?*

but

> *From the wide window towards the granite shore*
> *The white sails still fly seaward, seaward flying*
> *Unbroken wings.*

Conflict continues, and it is perhaps a sharper conflict than in the first poem: but it is also more fully resolved. The sights and sounds and smells for which the lost heart quickens to rebel are fresh and bracing. They are in contrast to the seductive scene which was visible through the slotted window of the third poem. Of course they too are a distraction from the main purpose and are disavowed, as representing the natural man's desire to assert the reality known to the senses, to feel himself 'substantial flesh and blood'. They are dreams and false, dreams out of the ivory gates of Greek legend. But the longing for the sea is satisfied in that the landscape of the 'higher dream' opens upon the sea which is God's will. 'And his will is our peace: it is that sea to which all moves that it createth and that nature maketh' (*Paradiso*, III, 85). The spirit of the fountain and the garden is also the spirit of the river and the sea.

There is in the last poem none of the sense of painful constriction which a critic has discerned in the first, where the 'I' seemed to be enclosed in the cell of self-knowledge. There is spaciousness: the poet faces the sea. 'Even among these rocks' must suggest desolation, but the rocks derive from the sea: there is no hint of despair in the last poem, but a sense of complete dependence which issues in the final supplication:

> *Teach us to sit still*
> *Even among these rocks*
> *Our peace is His will*
> *And even among these rocks*
> *Sister, mother*
> *And spirit of the river, spirit of the sea,*
> *Suffer me not to be separated*
> *And let my cry come unto Thee.*

E. E. Duncan Jones

It is characteristic of the technique of *Ash Wednesday* that the most poignant lines of the appeal:

> *Suffer me not to be separated*
> *And let my cry come unto Thee*

are not original expressions of religious feeling. 'Suffer me not to be separated from Thee' is a line from an ancient prayer, the *Anima Christi*, and the last line of all is part of the suffrages which the Church uses in many services: 'Lord, hear our prayer: and let our cry come unto Thee.'

Ash Wednesday is a poem of penance and preparation. By the time the end of the sequence is reached it is clear that there have been compensations for the face and voice which were renounced in the first part: but the face of the figure representing the new order of things is not seen, nor her voice heard: she is the 'silent sister veiled'. The end of *Ash Wednesday* looks out on to the sea: it is in *Marina* that 'the hope, the new ships' appear.

HELEN L. GARDNER

Four Quartets: A Commentary

THE PUBLICATION of the Quartets in one volume has made their interpretation easier in one way but more difficult in another. Read consecutively each illuminates the others, and the symbols employed become richer and more solid with repetition; but the cross-references between the poems are now seen to be so various, subtle and complex that formal interpretation seems more than ever clumsy and impertinent, and may even mislead readers, by appearing to impose a logical scheme on poems which continually escape from the logic of discourse into something nearer to the conditions of musical thought. But however difficult it may be to attempt an interpretation, and however unsatisfactory any interpretation is, it seems to be necessary with a poet so steeped in tradition as Mr Eliot and with poems so original in their form and manner. It need hardly be said that any interpretation bears about as much resemblance to the poems as a map does to a landscape, and like a map exists to be discarded by a walker who really knows the country. But a map is useful to strangers, and even to others it may suggest unfamiliar routes and places that have been overlooked.

The best kind of interpretation is that supplied by an author's other works, and this is particularly true of Mr Eliot, since he constantly repeats himself, as he himself owns—

> You say I am repeating
> Something I have said before. I shall say it again.
> Shall I say it again?

His poetry is extraordinarily self-consistent, and there is almost nothing he has published that does not form part of his poetic personality. One of the results of this integrity is that his later work interprets his earlier, as much as his earlier work does his

Helen L. Gardner

later; so that criticism of *The Waste Land* to-day is modified by *Ash Wednesday*, and *Ash Wednesday* is easier to understand after reading the Quartets. Mr Eliot's poetic career has shown to a high degree the quality that Keats called 'negative capability', when a man is 'capable of being in uncertainties, mysteries, doubts, without any irritable reaching after fact and reason'; he has never forced his poetic voice, but has been content with 'hints and guesses'. His readers must show the same patience. They must be ready to grow into knowledge of his poetry and to wait for Keats's moment when 'several things dovetailed in my mind'. This commentary will try to interpret the Quartets by the earlier works and by the reading that lies behind them, in order to help readers to that moment when they share with the poet the joy of apprehending significant relations.

The structure of the poems is seen very clearly when they are read together, and can be recognized as being essentially the same as the structure of *The Waste Land*. It is far more rigid than we should suspect from reading any one of the poems by itself. In fact, Mr Eliot has invented for himself, as the word Quartets suggests, a kind of poetic equivalent of 'sonata form', containing what are best described as five 'movements', each with an inner necessary structure, and capable of the symphonic richness of *The Waste Land* or the chamber-music beauties of *Burnt Norton*.[4] The five movements suggest the five acts of a drama, and the poems are built on a dialectical basis, employing deliberate reversals and contrasts in matter and style. This form seems perfectly adapted to its creator's way of thinking and feeling: to his desire to submit to the poetic discipline of strict law, and to his desire to find a form which gives him the greatest possible liberty in the development of a flexible, dramatic verse, and the greatest freedom in 'violently yoking together heterogeneous ideas'. The combination of an extreme apparent freedom with a great inner strictness corresponds to the necessities of his temperament.

[4] Cf. *The Music of Poetry*, 1942. 'I believe that the properties in which music concerns the poet most nearly, are the sense of rhythm and the sense of structure. . . . The use of recurrent themes is as natural to poetry as to music. There are possibilities for verse which bear some analogy to the development of a theme by different groups of instruments; there are possibilities of transitions in a poem comparable to the different movements of a symphony or a quartet; there are possibilities of contrapuntal arrangement of subject-matter'.

Four Quartets: A Commentary

The first movement in each of the Quartets consists of state-ment and counter-statement in a free blank verse. This must not be pressed too hard, for in *East Coker* the first movement falls into four parts, the statement and its contradiction being re-peated, in *The Dry Salvages* the metaphors of river and sea are more absolutely opposed than are the two paragraphs of *Burnt Norton*, while in *Little Gidding* the opposing statements of the first two paragraphs are blended in the third, the vivid par-ticularity of the scene in 'midwinter spring' and the assertion of unparticularity, the sameness of the experience, being summed up in the final phrase 'England and nowhere. Never and always'. But on the whole the opening movement is built on contradic-tions which the poem is to reconcile. The second movement shows the most striking similarities from poem to poem. It opens with a highly 'poetical' lyric passage—octosyllabics rhyming irregularly in *Burnt Norton* and *East Coker*, a simplified sestina in *The Dry Salvages* and three lyric stanzas in *Little Gidding*. This is immediately followed by an extremely colloquial passage, in which the idea which had been treated in metaphor and symbol in the first half of the movement is expanded, and given personal application, in a conversational manner. In the first three poems this is done in free blank verse, but in *Little Gidding* the metre employed is a modification of *terza rima*. Though the metre is regular and the style has a greater dignity, it still has colloquial force and the dialogue has the same per-sonal and topical reference as is found in the same section of the other poems. The third movement is the core of each poem, out of which reconciliation grows: it is an exploration, with a twist, of the ideas of the first two movements. In *Burnt Norton* the twilight world of the London Tube[5] 'neither plenitude nor vacancy' fades into the world of perpetual solitude. In *East Coker* there is a sudden shift in the emotions aroused by the word *darkness*, which gives point to the whole poem. In *The Dry Salvages* the change is a change of temper, from the reflective to the hortatory, and in *Little Gidding* the turn is from the personal and individual to the historic. The fourth movement is a lyric in all four poems. The fifth is again in two parts, but the change in

[5]In the first three poems, at this point, the image of passengers in a train is introduced. The 'place of disaffection' with 'men and bits of paper, whirled by the cold wind' in *Burnt Norton* is surely the London Tube.

manner and metre is slighter than in the second movement and it is reversed. Here the colloquial passage comes first, and then, without a feeling of sharp break, the rhythm tightens and the manner becomes graver for a kind of falling close. The whole movement recapitulates the themes of the poem, with personal and topical applications,[6] and makes a resolution of the discords of the first.

The Waste Land, if one allows for its much wider scope, dramatic method, and hosts of characters, follows the same pattern. *The Burial of the Dead* contains far more than two statements, but formally it is a series of contrasts of feeling towards persons and experiences. *The Game of Chess* opens with the elaborate description, in ornate style, of the lady at her dressing table, which contrasts violently, though not in its theme, with the talk of the women in the public-house. *The Fire Sermon*, the poem's heart, with its suffocating intensity, has moments when the oppression lifts, and a feeling of release and purification floods in. This twist is given by the evocations of another world: 'Et O ces voix d'enfants, chantant dans la coupole!', the 'inexplicable splendour of Ionian white and gold', the 'white towers', and the mingled emotions aroused by the word *burning*, for we remember not only St Paul's use of it to express the torment of desire, but also the brand plucked out, and the fire of the *Purgatorio*. The reference to the Buddha, the 'collocation of western and eastern asceticism', to which attention is drawn in the notes, anticipates the use of the *Bhagavad-gita* in *The Dry Salvages*. The fourth section is as always a brief lyric, and the fifth, while naturally being far more complex than the final movements of the later poems, fulfils the same function of resolution. Most people would agree to-day, in the light of Mr Eliot's later work, that the original critics of *The Waste Land* misread it, not recognizing it as an *Inferno* which looked towards a *Purgatorio*. Finding in it 'the disillusion of a generation', they failed to see in it what its treatment of history should have shown them, the disillusion of those in every generation, 'qui se haïssent et qui cherchent un être véritablement aimable'.

Burnt Norton, *East Coker*, *The Dry Salvages* and *Little Gidding* are poems on one theme, or rather on different aspects of the

---

[6] With the exception of *The Dry Salvages* all the poems open the fifth movement with a consideration of the nature of words and poetry.

same theme, and they are closely linked with *The Family Reunion*, which is a dramatic treatment of the subject. The theme can be variously defined, since we are speaking of poetry, not of philosophy or theology. It might be called the relation of time to eternity, or the meaning of history, or the redemption of time and the world of man. *The Family Reunion* emphasizes the idea of redemption, for Harry is seeking salvation and release from his sense of guilt. As he flies from the pursuing Eumenides, he is a man fleeing from the eternal, turning his back upon it to immerse himself in futile movement; when he recognizes them and accepts their summons, they become 'bright angels' and the ministers of his purgation. But this recognition springs out of his discovery of the past, his own and that of his family. As Agatha talks to him and tells him of his parents' unhappiness and sin, he at last understands the meaning of his own unhappy childhood and of his own marriage. He becomes then 'the consciousness of his unhappy family' and so can make expiation.[7]

The close connection of *The Family Reunion* with these poems will become apparent in the course of the discussion, but the themes had appeared in Mr Eliot's poetry before. They are made fully explicit in the choruses of *The Rock*, which contrast the determined and endless motion of the world of time with the stillness of eternity, and celebrate the union of time and eternity in

> *a moment in time and of time,*
> *A moment not out of time, but in time, in what we call history: transecting, bisecting the world of time, a moment in time but not like a moment of time,*
> *A moment in time but time was made through that moment: for without the meaning there is no time, and that moment of time gave the meaning.*

The same preoccupation with time is present in *Ash Wednesday*. In the fourth section the cry is heard, 'Redeem the time'. It is a common sundial motto and is appropriate there in a garden poem, as the memory of the phrase is at the opening of *Burnt*

[7] It is probable that the close of the play owes something to Bazin's *Life of Charles de Foucauld*. It is impossible for anyone who has read this book not to be reminded of it when Harry speaks of

> The worship in the desert, the thirst and deprivation,
> A stony sanctuary and a primitive altar,
> The heat of the sun and the icy vigil,
> A care over lives of humble people.

Helen L. Gardner

Norton. The problem of history and the time-process is one of the great themes of *The Waste Land*, where it is mingled with the desire for cosmic and personal salvation. No poem has ever shown a greater sense of the pressure of the past upon the present and of its existence in the present.

The problem of the time-process and its meaning is handled in the Quartets under different natural images and metaphors. All four poems have place-names for titles, two of them connected with Mr Eliot's family history. *Burnt Norton* differs from the others in having no field of reference, personal or historic. Its subject is a Cotswold manor house: merely a deserted house and garden which the poet has wandered into without knowing anything about the history of the house or who had lived in it. East Coker is a Somersetshire village from which in the seventeenth century Andrew Eliot set out for the New World. The Dry Salvages are a group of rocky islands off the coast of Massachusetts, part of the landscape of the poet's childhood, and part of the new experience of his ancestors after they had crossed the seas. Little Gidding is a village in Huntingdonshire to which in 1625 Nicholas Ferrar and his family retired in order to lead a common life of devotion. The starting point in all the poems is a landscape and the emotion and thought are bound up with a deeply felt sense of place.

Burnt Norton is a land-locked poem: its whole feeling is enclosed. It builds up, by suggestion, the picture of a house and formal garden. Its imagery is social and civilized, weighted with human history and culture. A formal garden is an admirable symbol for man's attempt to impose a pattern on his experience and to discipline nature. The picture gradually given here is of shrubbery and alley-walk, rose-garden, low box-borders and pool, sunflowers in the borders, clematis hanging from the wall and clipped yews. Within the house there are dried rose-leaves in a bowl, and there are references to a Chinese jar and to the music of the violin. All this is human and civilized, and the image used for reality is human too—the hidden laughter of children among the leaves of the garden.[8] This garden imagery of

---

[8]It has been suggested to me that the setting of the poem and the image of the laughing children hidden among the leaves may have been caught from Rudyard Kipling's *They*. The children there are both 'what might have been and what has been', appearing to those who have lost their children in the house of a blind woman who has never borne a child.

Four Quartets: A Commentary

Burnt Norton is used at the climax of *The Family Reunion*, in the dialogue between Harry and Agatha in the second scene of Part II. Agatha speaks there of 'looking through the little door, when the sun was shining on the rose-garden'. It is a moment of escape from the endless walking 'down a concrete corridor', or 'through the stone passages of an immense and empty hospital'. This moment of release from the deadening feeling of meaningless sequence—'in and out, in an endless drift', 'to and fro, dragging my feet'—into what is always present, the moment when, in Harry's phrase, 'the chain breaks' is the subject of *Burnt Norton*. The experience in the poem is pure of the tragic emotions of the play; it is an experience of a moment when one suddenly feels at home, accepted, free from anxiety, 'the practical desire'. It is not a moment that can be held, though it can be remembered. It is a moment which happens unexpectedly, as a grace, without the mind's preparing itself, or making any effort. The laughter of the children is a lovely surprise; 'sudden in a shaft of sunlight' comes 'the moment in and out of time'.

Burnt Norton does not suggest any dogma: its lyric movement, with its halting tentative rhythms, is purely natural in its theme and images. The subject of the poem is an experience for which theology provides an explanation and on which religion builds a discipline, the immediate apprehension of a timeless reality, felt in time and remembered in time, the sudden revelation of 'the one end, which is always present'. It is in the third section only that the poem suggests another way to the stillness at the heart of movement, by a deliberate descent into the world of perpetual solitude, the negative way. Christianity has found room in itself for both types of mystical experience, that which finds all nature a theophany, and that which feels the truth of Pascal's favourite text: 'Vere tu es Deus absconditus'. The way through the darkness is the subject of *East Coker*.

East Coker is much less confined in its setting; its background is a village and its environs, a landscape full of human history, but history of a ruder, less cultivated kind. It is set in a countryside where the sea is not far off, and the sea-wind can be felt. The first movement ends with a lightly touched reference to the sea; the sea provides an image of overwhelming desolation at the close of the second; and the final impulse of release and escape is given by the image of 'the vast waters of the petrel and the por-

Helen L. Gardner

poise'. The village is seen in its setting of open fields and the manor house is felt as part of the village, not a place private and walled-in. There is reference to the rhythm of the seasons and the farm. The metaphors used for reality are mostly non-human —the winter lightning, the wild strawberry, the whisper of running streams: the images of desolation are the dark wood, brambles and rocks.

In *The Family Reunion*, when Harry has become fully aware of the sin he has to expiate, he feels a sense of happiness and exclaims, 'This is like an end'; to which Agatha replies, 'And a beginning'. *East Coker* plays throughout with Mary Stuart's motto, 'In my end is my beginning', inverting it to a statement of rigid determinism at the opening, breaking it, and exploiting the various meanings of the word *end*. The final use of the phrase holds more than one meaning: *end* can mean death or the purpose for which we were created. The opening statement of the poem is determinist, and establishes by powerful rhythm and repetition the cyclic view of life and history. The life of man and of mankind and of the works of man is shown to be on the pattern of the life of the earth: all are an endlessly recurring succession of birth, growth, decay, and death. Contrasted, within the first movement, with the two statements of life as rhythm, pattern and sequence, are two passages in which the idea of stillness and rest is given. There is first the picture of the village sleeping in the hot silence of a late summer afternoon, and, at the close, the delicate hint of the breathless stillness of the dawn of a hot day. The notion of pattern and repetition leads only to despair: 'Feet rising and falling.' (This was Agatha's image for the sensation of imprisonment in time.) 'Eating and drinking. Dung and death.'

The lyrical passage with which the second movement opens contradicts both the rigid order and the stillness of the first. The idea of pattern is rejected, but so is the idea of peace. The seasons are all disordered. Spring thunder peals in November: the flowers of high summer jostle those of spring and winter. There is war too among the constellations, ending with the apocalyptic vision of the end of the world, burnt out to an icy cinder. But this romantic vision of chaos the poet rejects, for a plain, almost prosaic statement of the same chaos in the life of the individual. There too we find no ordered sequence, pattern or development. The metaphor of autumnal serenity is false

64

applied to man; experience does not bring wisdom, nor old age peace. The time when one knows never arrives, and the pattern is falsified by every new moment. We are always in the dark wood, in which Dante found himself in the middle of his life, the wood 'where the straight way is lost'. As we try to hold the past, it slips from us, engulfed in the darkness of the present.

The houses are all gone under the sea.
The dancers are all gone under the hill.

The third movement opens with this idea of darkness, with blind Samson's cry of anguish; but this anguish soon turns to a sombre triumph. The darkness, in which we are lost, swallows up and hides from us the base, the trivial and the ignoble, the meaningless pomps and vanities of the world. The poet rejoices in this victory of the dark in the same way as the writers of the early seventeenth century rejoiced in the levelling power of death. But this welcome to the darkness takes then another turn, and it is welcomed not only because it obliterates, but also because it reveals. Within the darkness is light; within the stillness, movement and dancing; within the silence, sound.

Mr Eliot is here writing in the tradition of those mystics who followed the negative way. It is a tradition that goes back beyond Christianity to the Neo-Platonists, who turned what had been a method of knowing—the dialectical method of arriving at truth by negations of the false—into a method of arriving at experience of the One. This doctrine of the ascent or descent ('the way up is the way down') into union with reality, by successively discarding ideas which would limit the one idea of Being, found a natural metaphor in darkness and night. It was a double-edged metaphor, since night expressed both the obliteration of self and all created things, and also the uncharacterized Reality which was the object of contemplation. The anonymous English mystic who wrote in this tradition in the fourteenth century used for his symbol a cloud, and called his book *The Cloud of Unknowing*. He taught that the soul in this life must be always between two clouds, a cloud of forgetting beneath, which hides all creatures and works, and a cloud of unknowing above, upon which it must 'smite with a sharp dart of longing love'. 'For all of other creatures and their works, yea, and of the works of God's self, may a man through grace have fullhead of knowing, and well he can think of them: but of God Himself can no man think. And

65

therefore I would leave all that thing that I can think, and choose
to my love that thing that I cannot think. For why: He may well
be loved, but not thought. By love may He be gotten and holden;
but by thought never.'

The actual phrase 'a cloud of unknowing' occurs in *The
Family Reunion*, and a line in *Little Gidding* comes directly from
the book, but in *East Coker* the great paradoxes of the negative
way are taken from its most famous doctor, St John of the Cross.
The riddling paradoxical statements at the close of the third
movement are an almost literal rendering of the maxims under
the 'figure' which stands as frontispiece to *The Ascent of Mount
Carmel* and which appear in a slightly different form at the close
of chapter 13 of the first book of that treatise.[9]   From this deliberately unpoetical close there is an abrupt transition to the
fourth movement with its majestic firmness of rhythm and
its powerful imagery.

The lyrical movement also unites despair and triumph, but
now in the contemplation of human pain. If to know you must
know nothing, then to live you must die. *East Coker* is far more
concerned with the response made to experience than *Burnt
Norton* is; and the experience to which response has to be made
is a tragic one, of loss and deprivation and homelessness. The
lyric, therefore, is a poem on the Passion, translated into the
metaphor of a hospital, and possibly suggested by Sir Thomas
Browne's phrase, 'For this world, I count it not an Inn, but an
Hospital; a place not to live, but to dye in'. The Passion is

[9]   In order to arrive at having pleasure in everything,
Desire to have pleasure in nothing.
In order to arrive at possessing everything,
Desire to possess nothing.
In order to arrive at knowing everything,
Desire to know nothing.
In order to arrive at that wherein thou hast no pleasure,
Thou must go by a way wherein thou hast no pleasure.
In order to arrive at that which thou knowest not,
Thou must go by a way that thou knowest not.
In order to arrive at that which thou possessest not,
Thou must go by a way that thou possessest not.
In order to arrive at that which thou art not,
Thou must go through that which thou art not.

(*The Complete Works of St John of the Cross*, translated by E. Allison Peers,
Vol. I, p. 63.)

thought of here not as a single historic event, but as an eternal
act perpetually operative in time, and it is linked with the
Eucharist. The grave heavy beat of the lines, the rigid stanza
form, the mood, the paradoxes, the sense of tragic triumph,
which the rhythm gives, make this lyric very like an early
Passion hymn:

> *Salve ara, salve victima,*
> *de passionis gloria,*
> *qua vita mortem pertulit*
> *et morte vitam reddidit.*

In the final movement, the feeling that every moment is a new
moment and a beginning, but that the past is alive in the
present, modifying it and being modified by it also, is at first
applied to the poet and the problems of expression and finally to
the life of the individual. The poem ends with the injunction to
be 'still and still moving', that we may pass through the 'dark cold
and the empty desolation' to the open waters of the sea, which
men have always regarded as a symbol of eternity. The close is
typical of the whole poem, at once terrifying and exalting.

The Dry Salvages has for its landscape the sea-coast of New
England; its dominant imagery is of rocks and the sea. This
landscape of his childhood Mr Eliot had used in the final section
of *Ash Wednesday*, looking on it there with longing, as on a world
hard to renounce. Of all three poems, *The Dry Salvages* is the
most beautifully integrated and marries most absolutely metaphor and idea. The sea imagery runs through it with a freedom
and a power hardly equalled in Mr Eliot's other poetry. He seems
to expatiate freely here and be at ease in nature.

The first movement is built on the contrast between two
metaphors, the river of life and the sea of life. The river is an
old metaphor for the life of man, and its flow from source to
mouth is linked here with the flow of the seasons from spring to
winter, and that of man's life from birth to death. The river is a
reminder of what we should like to forget, our bondage to
nature. Though it can for a time be ignored, it can assert its
power by catastrophe as well as by its inevitable progress. 'The
river is within us'; we feel it in our pulses. The sea is time of
another kind, the time of history, what Bacon meant when he
spoke of 'the vast seas of time'. Individual man launches himself
on this ocean of life and makes his short voyage, one of countless

similar voyages. 'The sea is all about us.' This metaphor of the
tossing seas of history denies both the cyclic view of history, the
biological interpretation, which imposes on events the rhythm
of a succession of rivers, each culture being first young and
vigorous, then mature, and finally decayed and outworn, and
also the doctrine of human progress, which finds in history an
upward development. We have instead a meaningless, perpetual
flux, a repetition without a pattern, to which each separate
voyage adds nothing but itself. But through the apparently in-
coherent restlessness of the sea, there is carried to our ears the
rhythm of the ground swell, different from the rhythm of the
river, which we hear in our heart-beats, coming from the very
depths of the ocean itself.

> And the ground swell, that is and was from the beginning,
> Clangs
> The bell.

The reminiscence of the doxology gives us the implication of the
symbol of the ground swell, which makes itself felt in our hearts
by the bell. The bell sounds a warning and a summons: it
demands a response. Like the bell of the Angelus it is a call to
prayer, and a commemoration of the mystery of the Incarnation;
like the bell at the consecration it is a call to worship and an-
nounces the presence of Christ; like the tolling bell it reminds
us of our death, and calls us to die daily.[10]

[10]The image of the sea-bell and the figures of the Eumenides in *The Family
Reunion* seem to me to hold the same meaning. Both are visitations of the
divine, messengers from eternity, terrifying till accepted. The underlying
meaning of both symbols is finely expressed by M. Francois Mauriac in a passage from *Dieu et Mammon*. M. Mauriac is also thinking of the Annunciation of
history and the annunciations of our individual lives and he too is linking the
summons with the sense of freedom in the soul. 'Aussi souverainement que
son Incarnation a partagé l'histoire humaine, Jésus-Christ cherche la seconde
propice pour s'insérer dans ce destin, pour s'unir à ce flot de chaque destinée
particulière, pour introduire sa volonté dans cette apparente fatalité, pour
détruire enfin cette fatalité. Tentatives quelquefois cachées et comme dé-
tournées, renouvelées à longs intervalles, souvent directes, impérieuses,
pressantes comme une occasion unique et solennelle, mais qui donnent
toujours à l'homme le plus asservi le sentiment qu'il demeure maître du oui
ou du non. Il a pu croire, à l'approche de la tentation trop connue, qu'aucune
force au monde ne l'empêcherait d'y succomber, et que ce péché familier
était vraiment l'acte qu'il ne dépendait pas de lui de ne pas commettre. Mais
voici que devant l'insistance de cette force qui demande à absorber sa faiblesse,
tout d'un coup, il se voit terriblement libre.'

Four Quartets: A Commentary

The sestina, with which the second movement opens, is a poem on these several annunciations. Under the metaphor of fishermen setting out on their perilous voyages, over 'an ocean littered with wastage', it pictures the lives of individual men, the sum of which makes history. It finds meaning in the process only in the union of the temporal with the eternal, in annunciations: the calamitous annunciation of terror and danger, the last annunciation of death, and the one Annunciation of history. The only *end* to the flux of history is man's response to the eternal. As in *The Waste Land*, it is 'by the awful daring of a moment's surrender' that we exist, by praying

> the hardly, barely prayable
> Prayer of the one Annunciation.

The meaningless monotony and pointless waste of living finds its purpose in the Virgin's words, 'Be it unto me according to Thy word'.

As in the other poems, the idea of the lyrical passage, given in metaphor and symbol, is then translated into the experience and idioms of every day. The past does not die; the visitations, particularly the visitations of anguish, are a perpetual experience, always recurring, preserved in memory and time. The whole of this passage reads like a commentary on the scene in *The Family Reunion* in which Agatha explains the past to Harry. It might have been written of Harry that he

> had the experience but missed the meaning
> And approach to the meaning restored the experience.

The pattern of the past is not a mere sequence, neither is it a development: if it were we could disown it and look to the future. But we cannot disown our past nor the past of others, nor the past of the human race; it lives within us and in moments of illumination it is restored to us.

The third movement turns to the future. Mr Eliot here introduces, as he had in *The Waste Land*, the scriptures of the East. He finds the same doctrine of response to what is always present in the *Bhagavad-gita*.[11] There Arjuna is concerned with the

---

[11]It might be objected, and it is an objection I feel strongly myself, that to introduce Krishna at this point is an error and destroys the poem's imaginative harmony. There is an unbridgeable gap between a religion that despairs of the material world and a religion that is built upon faith in an event by which the

problem of the innate sinfulness of action, and Krishna replies to his doubts by insisting on the necessity for disinterestedness. Man must not look for the fruits of action; he must live as if there were no future, as if every moment were the moment of death. The New Testament teaches a similar carelessness for the morrow, which was echoed in the choruses of *The Rock*.

Take no thought of the harvest, but only of proper sowing.

Here the future is at first thought as of something that already exists, as if it were already past, but not yet encountered, and the metaphor of the travellers, more lightly touched in the first two poems, is fully explored. First in the train, and then on the ocean, the travellers fare forward, bearing their past with them, and their future also, and yet in a real sense in a space between two lives. But to divide time harshly into past, present and future is to divide ourselves:

> *You are not the same people who left that station*
> *Or who will arrive at any terminus.*

Personality has meaning only in the present, in what we are. Our real destination is here; where we are going is where we are.[12]

The lyrical fourth movement is a prayer to Our Lady, and its

---

material world was not condemned but saved. It is in their view of history and the time-process that Christianity and Hinduism are most irreconcilably opposed; the incarnations of Vishnu give no significance to history, as does the unique Incarnation of Christian belief. But I feel I may be misunderstanding the intention of the poet in making this objection, since Mr Eliot himself in *After Strange Gods*, p. 40, makes rather this point in discussing modern cosmopolitanism. It is, perhaps, unkind to quote Mr Eliot against himself, but he has owned that two years' study of Sanskrit and 'a year in the mazes of Patanjali's metaphysics' left him 'in a state of enlightened mystification'. That is the feeling that this passage leaves with me.

[12]It is worth noting that the phrase

> this thing is sure,
> That time is no healer: the patient is no longer here,

echoes Pascal, while contradicting him: 'Le temps guérit les douleurs et les querelles, parce qu'on change, on n'est plus la même personne. Ni l'offensant, ni l'offensé, ne sont plus eux-mêmes' (*Pensées*, II, 122). Earlier in the same section Pascal had asserted the persistence of personality: 'Tout ce qui se perfectionne par progrès périt aussi par progrès, tout ce qui a été faible ne peut jamais être absolument fort. On a beau dire: *il est crû, il est changé*; il est aussi le même' (88). A reading of the *Pensées* would be a good general introduction to any study of Mr Eliot.

tender gravity and perfect fitness springs from the union in the
poem of idea and symbol. She is rightly prayed to in a poem of
the sea, because she is *Stella Maris*, to whom the fishermen and
their wives pray. She appears also, at the lyric climax, as the
handmaid of the Lord, who made the great response to the message of the angel, and as the mother of Christ, whose birth gives
meaning to time. She is also prayed to as *Mater Dolorosa*, for this
is a poem of sorrows, and the whole lyric takes up the theme of
the lovely melancholy sestina of the second movement; it recalls
the dangerous voyages, the 'ocean littered with wastage', and
over all

> the sound of the sea-bell's
> *Perpetual angelus.*

The fifth movement opens with a topical passage on the themes
of past and future, which men peer into for comfort and guidance,
turning to astrologers and fortune tellers, for reassurance about
the future which they dread, like the 'anxious worried women'
of the first movement, or turning to the past to explain the
present.

> *Men's curiosity searches past and future*
> *And clings to that dimension.*

Opposed to this search into past and future is 'the occupation of
the saint', the attempt to apprehend 'the point of intersection of
the timeless with time'. For the ordinary man, who is not a
saint, there are moments of illumination, 'hints and guesses'
upon which he founds his life of 'prayer, observance, discipline,
thought and action'. In these apprehensions of the eternal, preserved in memory, and fruitful beyond the moment in which
they were first felt, we find freedom from the tyranny of past and
future, and cease to feel ourselves the helpless victims of natural
forces. Because of this inner freedom, we can accept our temporal destiny and our bond with nature, the 'dung and death' to
which 'our temporal reversion' must return. In the 'hint half
guessed, the gift half understood', we find the meaning of our
own lives and the purpose of history. By this, time is redeemed
and is seen to be no enemy; for in time the world was made, in
time God was and is manifested, and, as Blake asserted in his
Marriage of Heaven and Hell, 'Eternity is in love with the pro-
ductions of time'.

Helen L. Gardner

In contrast with *The Dry Salvages*, which is peopled by the anonymous, the fishermen 'forever bailing, setting and hauling', the 'anxious worried women lying awake', the passengers settling for a journey, *Little Gidding* is full of particular destinies. The setting of the poem has a historical not a personal significance, and place and time are exactly defined. It is 'while the light fails on a winter's afternoon, in a secluded chapel'; and the poem is a record of a visit with a definite purpose: 'You are here to kneel where prayer has been valid'. We are not concerned with the 'hints and guesses' of the earlier poems, but with the life of 'prayer, observance, discipline, thought and action' of the last lines of *The Dry Salvages*. It is the actions of men, particularly their political actions, all that area of experience in which we are most aware of our freedom, which is the subject of meditation, things done rather than things suffered and endured. The thought of sin occurs here for the first time, not the sickness of the soul as in *East Coker*, but actual sin—'things ill done and done to others' harm'.

Little Gidding is a place of dedication, to which people came with purpose. It was not the ancestral home of the Ferrars, but a house which old Mrs Ferrar had bought the year before and to which the family went in the plague of 1624. In the next year Nicholas Ferrar 'grew to a full Resolution and determination of that thing and course of life he had so often wished for and longingly desired. And that week before Whitsunday gave himself to a very private Retirement, both in his thoughts and in his person, and was observed to fast much, eate sparingly and sleep little and on Whitsun Eve he was up all night in his study'. On Trinity Sunday he went with his tutor to see Laud, and was ordained deacon, refusing all his life to proceed to the priesthood, and returned to Little Gidding to share his goods with his family and to lead that life of ordered devotion and good works which made this remote Huntingdonshire village famous throughout England. An admirable picture of the life at Little Gidding can be found in Shorthouse's novel *John Inglesant*. It is a book of singular charm and refinement of feeling and all that is necessary for an understanding of what the name of the poem should suggest can be found in it. King Charles visited the community in 1633, and again during the troubled year of 1642, and legend says he came there for shelter by night, 'a broken king', after the final defeat of Naseby, just before he went north to give himself up to the Scots. Little Gidding is then a place of defeat. The community was scattered in 1647 and the chapel left ruined, and though the chapel was restored for worship in the nineteenth century, Nicholas Ferrar's ideal of a religious community based on the Christian family was never revived in the Anglican Church. Little Gidding remains 'a symbol perfected in death'.

The first movement of the poem is in three parts, but the transitions are not abrupt, and the third part is a kind of re-capitulation or development of the second, opening with the same phrase and coming round to a modification of the same conclusion. The first paragraph gives a vivid impression of the 'midwinter spring', the season that is 'not in time's covenant', a time of 'frost and fire' and 'blossom of snow'. The second paragraph asserts that at any time or any season this is a place of destiny, while the third brings us to the particular purpose here, which is prayer, and to the thought of the dead whose communication is 'tongued with fire beyond the language of the living'.

The beautiful lyric on decay, disintegration and death which opens the second movement recalls the imagery of the earlier poems. The 'burnt roses' and the 'dust in the air suspended' are from *Burnt Norton*, the 'wall, the wainscot and the mouse' from *East Coker*, the 'dead water and dead sand' from *The Dry Salvages*. The symbolism of the four elements which runs throughout the Quartets here reaches its fullest expression. The effect of the lyric is cumulative; human emotion and passion depart into the air, human effort crumbles into dust, the monuments of the human spirit are rotted by the corrosion of water and fire. The disintegration into the four elements whose mysterious union makes life finds its most poignant symbol in the final image of the gutted and water-logged ruins of 'sanctuary and choir'.

This theme of the 'death of hope and despair' and of the 'vanity of toil' underlies the colloquy that follows. Whereas in the other poems this section is a meditation, here, in keeping with the historical subject, we have an episode, a particular moment in time described. It is at dawn, between the departure of the last bomber and the sounding of the All Clear, and the scene is the streets of London. Instead of the poet's own reflections we have the conversation with the 'dead master', a communication from one whose 'concern was speech', and who in his day had his own 'thought and theory'. The setting, the style and above all the metre at once suggest *The Divine Comedy*. The stranger has the 'brown baked features' of Brunetto Latini (*Inferno xv*), and he ends his speech with the thought of the 'refining fire' of the *Purgatorio*, while his melancholy sense of supersession—'last season's fruit is eaten'—recalls the words of Oderisi (*Purgatorio xi*). But although the *Comedy* is full of interviews such as this, and in spite of the Dantean imagery and reminiscences, we are not to identify this 'familiar compound ghost' with Dante or with any other single poet. The ghost is 'both one and many'; he is 'intimate and unidentifiable'; he speaks of the experience of the poet in all ages and the fact that he adapts a line from Mallarmé and appears to recall a famous phrase of Virgil's[13] seems to depersonalize him rather than to suggest any identification. But the tone of the speech and some of the phrases recall strongly one great English poet, and that is Milton, the Milton of the close of *Paradise Lost*, of *Paradise Regained* and of *Samson*. It is Milton's melancholy picture of old age that we remember when we hear the disclosure of the 'gifts reserved for age'.

> Thou must outlive
> Thy youth, thy strength, thy beauty, which will change
> To withered weak and gray; thy Senses then
> Obtuse, all taste of pleasure must forgoe,
> To what thou hast.

And the close of the speech has a haunting Miltonic echo. 'I cannot praise a fugitive and cloistered virtue *unexercised* and unbreathed', wrote the confident Milton of 1644. The mood is very different and deeply troubled in *Paradise Regained* when political action is considered and in *Samson* where 'patience is the *exercise* of saints'. The weight of human suffering in Milton's later poetry, a touch of the scorn with which he cries 'What is glory but the blaze of fame', and the patience of his spirit seem to be suggested in this conversation in the disfigured streets of

[13]The line, 'To purify the dialect of the tribe', is a reminiscence of Mallarmé's 'Donner un sens plus pur aux mots de la tribu' (*Le Tombeau d'Edgar Allen Poe*). The contexts are so different that the reference does not illuminate the passage in *Little Gidding*. It appears to be a lovely line accidentally remembered for the precision of its definition of the poet's function.

I take it that the line, 'When I left my body on a distant shore', is a periphrasis for dying, the distant shore being the *ulterior ripa* of Virgil.

Four Quartets: A Commentary

London, and indeed Milton, whom Mr Eliot once found so anti-pathetic as a poet and a man, is very much in mind throughout the poem. The reference is explicit in the next section where along with Strafford, Laud and Charles who died on the scaffold, the poet remembers 'one who died blind and quiet';[14] and though the words are not Milton's the repeated 'all shall be well' cannot but remind us of the conclusion of Milton's last poem, the final chorus of *Samson*.

> *All is best, though we oft doubt,*
> *What th' unsearchable dispose*
> *Of highest wisdom brings about*
> *And ever best found in the close.*

After the grave melancholy of the second movement the third opens with a tone of confidence and in a rhythm that is almost gay. The beautiful imagery of the first movement is recalled in the metaphor of the hedgerow and the change in human beings from attachment to detachment is thus felt to be something natural occurring in the proper course of things. Between these two states 'unflowering' is the detachment of the Stoics or of the Gnostic *illuminati*, the sterile apparent freedom from desire of those who have never felt love. These general reflections on the pattern of our individual lives yield to the thought of the pattern of history, where we can feel a unity between men who in a 'warlike various and tragical age' found themselves opposed. At the turn of the movement and again at its close and at the close of the whole poem, which is also the close of the series, Mr Eliot has set the mysterious words of Julian of Norwich.[15] Dame Julian, whom some think the greatest of the medieval English mystics, received sixteen 'shewings' in the year 1373,

[14]'Hee dy'd', wrote Milton's nephew, John Phillips, 'in a fitt of the Gout, but with so little pain or Emotion, that the time of his expiring was not perceiv'd by those in the room. And though hee had bin long troubl'd with that disease, insomuch that his Knuckles were all callous, yet was hee not ever observ'd to be very impatient.'

[15]There is an appropriateness in Mr Eliot's use of Dame Julian for the medieval English mystics were much loved in the seventeenth century, par-ticularly, of course, by those 'who died forgotten in other places abroad', the exiled Romanists. Dame Julian was printed in a modernized edition in 1670 by Serenus de Cressy, once fellow of Merton and Chaplain to Falkland, later a Benedictine at Douai. Cressy appears in *John Inglesant* at a moving moment in the story to urge on Inglesant the claims of the monastic life.

which she wrote down and amplified and explained fifteen years later. Her revelations were of the Passion and of words spoken to her from the Cross. In her thirteenth revelation she was much troubled by the thought of the origin of sin in a world created by infinite Goodness, but the voice which spoke to her said: 'Sin is behovable, but all shall be well, and all shall be well, and all manner of things shall be well', and in her fourteenth revelation concerning prayer she heard the words: 'I am Ground of thy Beseeching'. For fifteen years, as she tells us, she pondered on the meaning of what she had heard and seen, and she was at last answered: 'Wouldst thou learn thy Lord's meaning in this thing? Learn it well: Love was His meaning. Who shewed it thee? Love. What shewed He thee? Love. Wherefore shewed it He? For Love. Hold thee therein and thou shalt learn and know more in the same. But thou shalt never know or learn therein other thing without end.'

This Love is the theme of the lyric movement. The fires which have flamed and glowed throughout the poem here break out and declare their nature. Man cannot help loving; his choice is between the fire of self-love and the fire of the love of God. The 'dark disordered fire of our soul', as William Law wrote, 'can as well be made the foundation of Heaven as it is of Hell. For when the fire and strength of the soul is sprinkled with the blood of the Lamb, then its fire becomes a fire of light, and its strength is changed into a strength of triumphing love, and will be fitted to have a place among those flames of love that wait about the throne of God'. As *East Coker* has at this point a lyric on the eternal Passion, *Little Gidding* celebrates the eternal Pentecost, the perpetual descent of the Dove in tongues of fire.

The assurance and serenity of the final movement crowns the whole sequence. The line dividing its two paragraphs, which comes from the second chapter of *The Cloud of Unknowing*, makes explicit the meaning of the 'moment in the rose-garden', the bell heard beneath the waves, and the 'communication of the dead'. History is the field of the operation of the Spirit; it is a 'pattern of timeless moments'; the historic moment, the moment of choice is always here. We are back again at the close in the garden of *Burnt Norton*, passing through the first gate into our first world, and the children are there in the appletree. Effort and exploration are forgotten in the sense of the given; living is the discovery of the already known, and beginning and end are one. All shall be well, when all is gathered in love, and the rose, the symbol of natural beauty and natural love, is one with the fire, the love by which all things are made. *Little Gidding* is a poem of fire, the fire which is torment to the self-loving, purgation to the penitent, and ecstasy to the blessed, and it closes with mortal and immortal life united in the resurrection symbol of the rose of heaven. 'And I saw full surely', wrote Dame Julian at the close of her book, 'that ere God made us He loved us; which love was never slacked, nor ever shall be. And in this love He hath done all His works; and in this love He hath made all things profitable to us; and in this love is our life everlasting. In our making we had beginning; but the love wherein He made us was in Him without beginning: in which love we have our beginning. And all this shall we see in God, without end'.

B . R A J A N

The Unity of the Quartets

THE QUARTETS have now been before the public for some time and it is impossible not to recognize that they constitute a unity. That unity is one in which no element is eventually definable except in relation to the experience which is given by the whole. The assurance of *Little Gidding* is contributed to by the questionings of *Burnt Norton*. But to isolate the presiding organization, the purpose and plan by which the elements are tempered, is difficult and, one can argue, unprofitable. The facts are destroyed by being disentangled. The study of the law, the pattern, by itself, is a degradation of the whole which it informs. Thus at the outset, the rights of the critic are challenged. He cannot analyse because he will kill by analysis. He cannot generalize because there are no categories more general than those which are constructed in *Burnt Norton*. He cannot transpose or represent, because if he does so his inferior imitation will fade in the presence of the poetic fact.

The alternative is to define, like Mr Eliot, by exclusion. In such circumstances the aim of the critic should be not so much to reformulate, as to suggest by analogy, to strike from the circumference to a central faith by a sensitive examination of what that faith entails. There are various points on the circle at which one could usefully begin, but it strikes me that one of the most direct ways of finding out what Mr Eliot is trying to do is to find out what he thinks of the language which is his medium. The Quartets have much to say about language and what is said makes it clear that the changes of attitude reflected in these comments have a symbolic as well as a technical significance. In the first place the location of the passages is important. They invariably turn up in section five and their relatively loose colloquial rhythms precede a kind of reconciling *coda* in which the antitheses generated by the poem are temporarily overcome.[16] These resolutions within the unit of the poem can be located in turn within the scheme of the tetralogy. Hence the digressions fulfil a double purpose. Like every other item in the poems they reflect the dominant colouring of the part and at the same time help to illuminate and define the details of movement within the pattern of the whole.[17]

Thus, in keeping with the abstract, exploratory character of *Burnt Norton*, the treachery of words is felt as something impersonal and external. It points by implication to the stability of 'the Word' attacked 'by voices of temptation', but it appears as if detached from any specific experience. There is not yet as in *East Coker* 'the intolerable wrestle with words and meanings'. The categories and concepts have been constructed but it is only in the following poems that they are applied to widening horizons of inquiry. In *East Coker*, as I have suggested, the conflict is more specific and it is this which enables Eliot to suggest that feelings as well as words are imprecise, that 'the shabby equipment' which constitutes our language is after all appropriate to our 'undisciplined squads of emotion'. In *The Dry Salvages* there is no equivalent 'digression'. The omission is necessary because the climax of the Incarnation is different in kind from those which follow or precede it. It is the central, dynamic affirmation through which the solutions constituted by each of the poems are ordered and given significance. Being thus unique it must be uniquely revealed. But the 'temporal reversion' it makes possible, the return to the specific, localized facts of nature, is transfigured by experience at the level of grace. So in the language of *Little Gidding*, the language which registers this wholeness, there can exist no conflict between the symbol and the fact.

> And every phrase
> And sentence that is right (where every word is at home,
> Taking its place to support the others,
> The word neither diffident nor ostentatious,
> An easy commerce of the old and the new,

[16]See Miss H. L. Gardner's 'Four Quartets: A Commentary' (pp. 57-62 of this volume) for details of the formal organization.

[17]See *Burnt Norton*, V.
> The detail of the pattern is movement
> As in the figure of the ten stairs.

The common word exact without vulgarity,
The formal word precise but not pedantic,
The complete consort dancing together)
Every phrase and every sentence is an end and a beginning.

The development I have traced can be differently[18] suggested. One could compare time, the abstract, 'eternally present' time of *Burnt Norton* with the ceremonial, hierarchic time of *East Coker* (there is a time for building/And a time for living and for generation).[19] There is the ground swell of *The Dry Salvages* 'older than the time of chronometers'. There is the time of *Little Gidding* 'a symbol perfected in death', an understanding which points to the eternal truth of history.

The moment of the rose and the moment of the yew-tree
Are of equal duration. A people without history
Is not redeemed from time, for history is a pattern
Of timeless moments.

These examples (I leave it to the reader to find others) make it apparent that there is a common scheme which underlies the deployment of each symbol. What this scheme is I should hesitate to specify, beyond suggesting that *Burnt Norton* is concerned with constructing concepts, *East Coker* and *The Dry Salvages* with the application of those concepts to a steadily widening area of experience, and *Little Gidding* with the transfiguration of the facts within that area, by the radiance and finality of a truth which lies beyond it. This sequence will serve as a means of classification, but only with the reservation that, in the poem itself, it exists and is justified as a poetic necessity. What we see as a structure is transmitted as a movement. The organization far from being assumed is inexorably entailed. It is not a concession which you charitably make, but a conclusion to which you are unavoidably driven.

To appreciate best how this progression is achieved we have to examine the imagery of the poetry. *Burnt Norton*, as I have pointed out, is concerned with establishing concepts. Now if this

[18]This development is summarized in *The Rock*:
Out of the sea of sound the life of music
Out of the slimy mud of words, out of the sleet and hail of verbal imprecisions
Approximate thoughts and feelings, words that have taken the place of thoughts
and feelings
There springs the perfect order of speech and the beauty of incantation.

[19]The passage recalls Ecclesiastes iii.

process is to be poetically important, if it is to be anything more than the versification of a philosophical inquiry, the concepts which emerge must be poetically real, commanding and compelling one's attention, imposing themselves on the data they are meant to interpret. There are two ways in which this can be done. The poetry can weaken our allegiance to facts by dissociating them from their conventional properties; and it can strengthen our allegiance to ideas by the rhythmic power which it brings to their assertion. Observe for instance the opening of *Burnt Norton*:

> Time present *and* time past
> *Are both perhaps* present *in* time future,
> *And* time future *contained in* time past.
> *If* all time *is eternally* present
> All time *is unredeemable*.

The repetition, the strong stressed rhythm, the positioning of key words and the evocations of 'future' and 'past' bind together the ideas of eternity, time, and presence. The taut scholastic diction held back from certainty by the donnish 'perhaps' underlines the assurance of 'unredeemable', and the emotions it evokes are reflected on the next line—'What might have been is an abstraction'. It is not just a matter of saying with Aquinas that even God cannot undo the past. 'Abstract' used evocatively (unreal abstractions) stresses the presence and reality of the eternal. In so doing it is fortified by the recessional effect of 'echo'—'my words echo/Thus, in your mind'—and as the poetry shifts from thoughts to physical objects our response is determined by these emotional preselectors. In contrast the poetry of the concrete is deliberately and insistently evasive.

> *There they were, dignified, invisible,*
> *Moving without pressure, over the dead leaves,*
> *In the autumn heat, through the vibrant air.*

Here we have 'invisible' pitted against the solidity of 'dignified', 'dead' opposed to 'vibrant', and the paradoxes of 'moving without pressure' and 'autumn heat'. This in itself is inconclusive—Eliot in *Little Gidding* can talk triumphantly of 'Midwinter spring'—but the rhythm itself, shifting, delicate, and marked by a lavish employment of caesuras, helps to sustain what is suggested by the diction.[20] Even the flowers in this universe are unnatural. 'There they were as our guests, accepted and accepting.' In this sixteenth-century house with its bowl of rose leaves, its Chinese jar, and its corridors that seem to recede into vagueness we grasp eagerly at what we think are facts—'Dry the pool, dry concrete, brown-edged'. But even this is denied us—'The pool was filled with water out of sunlight'. The effect of this dissociation, this remoteness, is to emphasize the superior reality of the pattern. The boarhound and the boar, despite their symbolic implications, belong, by comparison, to an immediate foreground of fact. Similarly 'the still point of the turning world' does not seize your imagination because it is transcendental. You accept it for quite the opposite reason because it is the most concrete thing the poetry has produced. Mr Eliot has succeeded brilliantly in his main preoccupation which is to make philosophic terms more solid and tangible than objects.[21] At the same time, by limiting the experience from which he has built his concepts, by confining it to a sixteenth-century house he has, as it were, left uncharted areas of feeling in which the validity of these concepts can be verified. In the simplest of senses *East Coker* and *The Dry Salvages* are poems of spiritual exploration.

The setting for *East Coker* is a village not far from the sea. The imagery of the poem is more photographic than that of *Burnt Norton* and the pattern it comprehends is less remote. It is based on an order that springs from nature, from the processes of the seasons and of living. But it is unstable, enduring only 'if you do not come too close'. The quotation from Eliot's *Gouernour* which

[20] To justify the unusual importance I attach to rhythm I should like to quote from *The Music of Poetry*. 'I know that a poem, or a passage of a poem, may tend to realize itself first as a particular rhythm before it reaches expression in words, and that this rhythm may bring to birth the idea and the image; and I do not believe that this is an experience peculiar to myself.'

[21] I can recall only one point at which a relatively compelling rhythm is associated with the kind of imagery we would normally call concrete. It is in section 4,

> After the kingfisher's wing
> Has answered light to light, and is silent, the light is still.

Here the scintillation is achieved by repeating *li*, inverting it in 'silent', reinverting it, and arriving finally at the stability of 'st*ill*'. But even this suggests the opposite of permanence.

follows this line is thrown into prominence by the archaic spelling. By being thus subtly foreign to its context it accentuates the disequilibrium which the previous lines assert. The laughter of the dancers is therefore not spontaneous. It is the 'mirth of those long since under earth', a gesture cut off from the experience which gives it validity. The images lapse into vacancy, the vacancy of interstellar spaces, of underground trains and operating tables, and, in section four, into an ironic and somewhat overworked presentation of the earth as a hospital in which the patients are cured by sickness. The breakdown of traditional criteria in this chaos is presented both indirectly—'The dancers are all gone under the hill'—and as an explicit statement.

> There is, it seems to us,
> At best, only a limited value
> In the knowledge derived from experience.
> The knowledge imposes a pattern, and falsifies,
> For the pattern is new in every moment
> And every moment is a new and shocking
> Valuation of all we have been.

The past is irrelevant as a means of judging the present. The sense of history, of kinship and community in time, can no longer interpret the urgencies which drive us. The first response is bewilderment—'as we grow older/The world becomes stranger, the pattern more complicated'. But this disintegration of a vital and ceremonial order, this growing complexity and strangeness in experience, demands not a cessation but an expansion of enquiry. The way out is 'through the dark cold and the empty desolation' and the sea which haunts the universe of *East Coker*, 'the vast waters of the petrel and the porpoise', becomes in *The Dry Salvages* the ground swell and the underlying menace driving and enduring through the processes of history.[22]

I know no poem more terrifying than *The Dry Salvages*. It touches the nadir of disillusion. People who think otherwise, who argue wistfully about a golden age of scepticism in *The Waste Land*, have simply not read the sestines of section two. In *The Dry Salvages* the limits of exploration are reached. There are

[22] As 'houses' links *Burnt Norton* and *East Coker*, the sea *East Coker* and *The Dry Salvages*, so also the phrase 'temporal reversion' links *The Dry Salvages* to *Little Gidding*. Finally the last lines of *Little Gidding* return us to the beginnings of *Burnt Norton*.

no reservations to qualify analysis. There is not, as in *Burnt Norton*, a house, a universe which is accepted as eternal. There are not, as in *East Coker*, houses that live and die but which are held together by a present and suffering ego. There are neither refuges from nor barriers to experience. There is only honesty to face and conquer the fact. The clang of the opening sentence of *The Dry Salvages* is unlike anything that has gone before.

> *I do not know much about gods; but I think that the river*
> *Is a strong brown god—sullen, untamed and intractable.*

How different this is from the precise yet tentative beginnings of *Burnt Norton*—'Time present and time past/Are both perhaps present in time future'. How different from the ceremonial, incantatory cadences of *East Coker*—'Old stone to new building, old timber to new fires/Old fires to ashes, and ashes to the earth'. The resonant n's, the towering monosyllables are symptomatic of a new dimension. The latent menace of 'unhonoured, unpropitiated' seems to gain force from the succeeding cliché. The artifice of men is powerless against it—'His rhythm was present in the nursery bedroom/In the rank ailanthus of the April dooryard'. The self itself cannot endure against it—'The river is within us, the sea is all about us'. The line with its swirling, eddying ryhthms threatening to fall apart while the internal half rhymes precariously hold it together helps to reiterate this looming instability. The time which is measured by the bell 'under the oppression of the silent fog' is a time stripped of human specifications, an alien, pulsing and ultimate reality living through all thought and permeating all action.

Section two carries the disintegration further. The passage is as intricately organized as anything Eliot has written, but one feels that its elaborate discipline is only accepted so that the chaos it carries may be poetically endurable. The listless hypermetric endings trail over an eternal emptiness. The first stanza widens the universe of pain—it is the shock of 'soundless wailing' which suggests that flowers too may suffer—and its insistent repeated 'ings' establish an undertone of meaningless accumulation which the second stanza makes explicit.

> *There is no end, but addition : the trailing*
> *Consequence of further days and hours.*

Even the renunciation of 'what was believed in as the most

reliable' can impose no pattern on this alien flux. It brings only the incoherence of 'unattached devotion' a 'drifting boat' with no anchor in infinity. The crescendo at the end of this stanza is superbly contrived. The key is, of course, the sequence of n's which drive to a climax in 'clamour', but the sudden flare of sound which is thus achieved reflects back on 'silent' as if to diminish its stature and to emphasize the helplessness of the individual against the unintelligible forces which control him. Once reached, the *forte* is sustained through two stanzas by a more liberal use of explosive consonants. Despair expands to a complete denial of hope—'We cannot think of a time that is oceanless'. In this surrounding, stifling, unremitting hostility you can survive only by appealing to an inner will to coherence.

> *We have to think of them as forever bailing,*
> *Setting and hauling, while the North East lowers.*

The diminuendo ebbs into numbness. When flowers have withered there is still no end to their withering. It seems almost as if, in the face of his hostility, there is nothing more that one can honestly say. Yet from the fact and sinew of the poetry itself, from the forces which generate and sustain this chaos, from that music of reality which endures when the momentary agony which wields it is forgotten, from the facts thus nakedly and inescapably presented there arises the assurance which is eventually to redeem them. The 'unprayable prayer' of the first stanza becomes the 'hardly, barely prayable' prayer of the sixth. It is that progression, urged and incipient in the music, which enables the poem to say what it must in the teeth of all that it has declared and demonstrated.

> *It seems, as one becomes older,*
> *That the past has another pattern, and ceases to be a mere sequence.*

But if the spiritual crisis is over, the technical problem remains. It is very creditable to say that ripeness is all. But if an assertion like this is to be convincing, if Mr Eliot is not to end by joining the Devil's party, the lyricism of doubt must be surpassed and transformed by the poetry of acceptance.[23] It is this

---

[23]'. . . . every man who thinks and lives by thought must have his own scepticism, that which stops short at the question, that which ends in denial, or that which leads to faith and which is somehow integrated into the faith which transcends it. And Pascal as the type of one believer, which is passionate

tremendous responsibility which the rest of the tetralogy undertakes. The start is none too happy; the descent into the everyday which terminates in 'even a very good dinner' is no doubt deliberate. But it is not inevitable and its homeliness is too startling to blend happily with its context. But the failure such as it is (and it is only momentary) is amply atoned for by the commanding insistence of the lines which follow.

> We had the experience but missed the meaning,
> And approach to the meaning restores the experience
> In a different form, beyond any meaning
> We can assign to happiness. I have said before
> That the past experience revived in the meaning
> Is not the experience of one life only
> But of many generations'[4]

It is no accident that the word 'meaning' is used for the first time in the tetralogy. The assertion of a standard not given by experience demands the use of a concept not hitherto given by the poetry. But this is balanced by the reservation—which Mr Eliot makes clear enough—that the meaning does not transcend the experience it interprets. It is latent in what we recognize as fact. But it can be discovered only in the act of faith, the 'sudden illumination' which isolates the pattern in which present and past are significantly related. That pattern is not one of development, of a present which contains all that is important in the past. It is not the abstraction of recorded history, looking over its shoulder to the terror it suppresses. It is an understanding, a total tolerance, in which evil and perversity are endured for the sake of the insight they ultimately generate. The basis of that insight is not merely self-denial, for self-denial has to assume self-consciousness. It is founded on something more delicate and

---

and ardent, but passionate only through a powerful and regulated intellect, is in the first sections of his unfinished Apology for Christianity facing unflinchingly the demon of doubt which is inseparable from the spirit of belief' ('The Pensées of Pascal', Essays Ancient and Modern, London, 1936, pp. 150-1).

[24]The repetition and the persistent stressing of key-words recall the first few lines of Burnt Norton. The coming together into a new significance is supported emotionally by 'revived' and 'restored'; it is this combined with the sense of new life in 'meaning' which makes the upswing technically possible. Mr Eliot's control in the use of key-words is remarkable. 'History' is only used once before Little Gidding and 'eternity' is never used at all if we ignore 'eternally' in the fourth line of Burnt Norton.

difficult, namely on the abandonment of the self as the climax and measure of reality. To realize that assumption one has to begin by admitting that the suffering of others is more real than one's own.

> . . . our own past is covered by the currents of action,
> But the torment of others remains an experience
> Unqualified, unworn by subsequent attrition.

A few words later on Mr Eliot can say categorically—'the agony abides', and there is involved no assumption of clenched and stoic endurance. 'Time the destroyer is time the preserver.' 'The sombre season' with its 'core of fierce destruction'[25] provides no pretext for sympathy or complaint. It is a disinterestedness supremely human, yet beyond the working limitations of humanity, a freedom beyond the 'practical desire', a strength which knows truth because it has lived through damnation. In the rasping, abiding savagery of these last lines there is neither bitterness nor vehemence, only a crystal clear acceptance of reality as it is.

Section three begins badly. Mr Eliot is never happy in 'the maze of Oriental metaphysics' and his wanderings this time are uncomfortably sinuous

> I sometimes wonder if that is what Krishna meant—
> Among other things—or one way of putting the same thing:
> That the future is a faded song, a Royal Rose or a lavender spray
> Of wistful regret for those who are not yet here to regret,
> Pressed between yellow leaves of a book that has never been opened.

I do not doubt that it is possible to defend this passage. There are ambiguities, complexities and an ingenious associational circuit, to say nothing of the device of describing the future in the language of the past. But Mr Eliot is too good a poet to play the virtuoso. Intricacy of this kind is uncomfortably close to Berowne's 'Light seeking light doth light of light beguile', and to my mind it cannot compare with the grave declamatory cadences of the second half of this section, a beauty of insight which quietens as it commands

> Fare forward, you who think that you are voyaging;
> You are not those who saw the harbour
> Receding, or those who will disembark.

[25] The phrase is of course from Keats.

B. Rajan

Swiftly and economically the section moves to its climax. Reality is something seen through the eyes of death and the action thus generated by a death enduring through every moment is 'the one action . . . /Which shall fructify in the lives of others'. The symbolism anticipates 'a lifetime's death in love' and is a direct progression from the recognition of the supreme reality of other people's suffering which was established and asserted in section two. Krishna's noble admonition—'Not fare well,/But fare forward'—is followed by the fourth section which perhaps owes something to the sermon in *Moby Dick*. If the reference to Jonah is intended, Matthew xii, 40, also comes aptly and this hushed and haunting invocation then leads on naturally to the climax of the poem. But whatever repose we may have won to is rudely shattered by the succeeding harangue:

> *To communicate with Mars, converse with spirits. . . .*

But this descent into Suburbia has its uses. Whirled helter skelter in a limbo of tea leaves we see these malpractices pointing to one necessity. Mr Eliot gesticulates spaciously—'Whether on the shores of Asia or in the Edgware Road'—and now with no further prevarication the verse leaps up to its 'great argument'.

> *Men's curiosity searches past and future*
> *And clings to that dimension. But to apprehend*
> *The point of intersection of the timeless*
> *With time, is an occupation for the saint—*
> *No occupation either, but something given*
> *And taken, in a lifetime's death in love,*
> *Ardour and selflessness and self-surrender.*

The confidence of the poetry is superb. It disdains analogies. It will have nothing to do with snapshot imagery. The resonant pride of those polysyllables summons all fact to a defining judgement and then, as the sibilants slow its clash and recoil, the open vowels hush it to repose. Against that liberating assurance the verse speaks again melodious and human:

> *For most of us, there is only the unattended*
> *Moment, the moment in and out of time,*
> *The distraction fit, lost in a shaft of sunlight,*
> *The wild thyme unseen, or the winter lightning*
> *Or the waterfall, or music heard so deeply*
> *That it is not heard at all, but you are the music*
> *While the music lasts.*

The Unity of the Quartets

Mr Scarfe refers delightedly to this passage as 'crammed with references to sensual experience' and contrasts Eliot's precision with MacNeice's vagueness.[26] Such a procedure seems to me to impose quite the wrong demands upon the poetry. In fact the imagery is inexact—deliberately so, because what Mr Eliot has to say cannot be said pictorially. The effect depends on disparate 'hints and guesses' reaching to the paradox of music that is not heard and rising from thence to the truth of Incarnation. About this progression I will not stop to argue. Mr Eliot means what is meant by any Christian and it should be clear that the experience behind the second half of The Dry Salvages is meant to suggest that of spiritual rebirth.[27] But I shall have failed completely if I cannot persuade the reader that the symbol is one which the poetic inquiry *demands* for its fulfilment. It is important to many that it is theologically orthodox. For the critic, what matters is that it is poetically inevitable, that from the upswing from chaos in section two every phrase and every sentence has moved towards this destiny. The lines which follow are sombre, but they

[26] *Auden and After* (London, 1942), pp. 62-7. Eliot has made it quite clear that he is not trying to provide arresting imagery or 'references to sensual experience'. In 1933 he said at New Haven '. . . to write poetry which should be essentially poetry, with nothing poetic about it, poetry standing naked in its bare bones, or poetry so transparent that we should not see the poetry, but that which we are meant to see through the poetry, poetry so transparent that in reading it we are intent on what the poem *points at*, and not on the poetry, this seems to me the thing to try for' (Matthiessen, *The Achievement of T. S. Eliot*, London, 1935, p. 90). Eliot repeats this in 1938. 'The poetry is something to be looked through not *at*' (*The Townsman*, July 1938, p. 10). In 1940 he says, in referring to Yeats, 'What is necessary is a beauty which shall not be in the line or isolable passages but woven into the dramatic texture itself; so that you can hardly say whether the lines give grandeur to the drama or whether it is the drama which turns words into poetry' (*Purpose*, July 1940). In 1942 he says it again. 'The great poet's craft may sometimes fail him: but at his greatest moments he is doing what Kipling is doing on a lower plane—writing transparently so that our attention is directed to the object and not to the medium' (*A Choice of Kipling's Verse*, London, 1942, Intro., pp. 14-15). Yet, despite all this, Scarfe's criteria stand, consciously or unconsciously, at the back of most modern criticism of Eliot.

[27] I take for granted that Christian revelation is the only full revelation ; and that the fullness of Christian revelation resides in the essential fact of Incarnation, in relation to which all Christian revelation is to be understood. The division between those who accept, and those who deny, Christian revelation I take to be the most profound difference between human beings' (*Revelation*, edited John Baillie and Hugh Martin, London, 1937, pp. 1-2).

are not depressing. Falling away from the 'sudden illumination' they sink down into a massive earthy solidity reassuringly stable in its drab but settled repose.

> We, content at the last
> If our temporal reversion nourish
> (Not too far from the yew-tree)
> The life of significant soil.

Little Gidding is the record of that temporal reversion. The fact may seem obvious but it helps us to identify the timbre and quality of the poem's music. Here more than anywhere else 'the intellect is at the tips of the senses' and the crude materials of everyday events, the pigsty, the dull facade and the tombstone are raised and refined into symbolic dignity.

> Midwinter spring is its own season
> Sempiternal though sodden towards sundown,
> Suspended in time, between pole and tropic.
> When the short day is brightest, with frost and fire,
> The brief sun flames the ice, on pond and ditches.

I have emphasized words which are antithetical because this strangely stable reconciliation of opposites is throughout characteristic of Little Gidding. 'The impossible union of spheres of existence' is implied persistently by what the poetry does. Mr Eliot has used this method before notably in his incidental images.

> The menace and caress of wave that breaks on water

Or again

> Out at sea the dawn wind
> Wrinkles and slides.

But in Little Gidding, for the first time, it is made part of a uniform current of assertion, independent of particular moods and contexts.

> Both one and many; in the brown baked features
> The eyes of a familiar compound ghost
> Both intimate and unidentifiable

Or in the grating forthrightness of

> First, the cold friction of expiring sense
> Without enchantment, offering no promise
> But bitter tastelessness of shadow fruit

Always the rhythm confident, decisive, finding assurance

where *Burnt Norton* found denial, surges to a common truth in which all differences are unified. The statement of the law may sometimes be explicit.

> *If you came this way,*
> *Taking any route, starting from anywhere,*
> *At any time or at any season,*
> *It would always be the same:*

Sometimes it is clothed in vernal, lingering tenderness

> *Now the hedgerow*
> *Is blanched for an hour with transitory blossom . . .*
> *If you came this way in may time, you would find the hedges*
> *White again, in May, with voluptuary sweetness.*

But always it is there, a continuous affirmation, which the sway and movement of the poetry sustains. The verse is earth bound, but it is never imprisoned. It sees eternity as flesh and blood. It watches abstract definitions 'flourish in the same hedgerow'. The church at the world's end, the symbol that links eternity and time, is steeped too in the associations of seventeenth-century history, the abiding, permeating humanity of events. For *Little Gidding* is a poem about history, history felt as real in one's bones. a vitality drawn from the power of the past which liberates one for action in the present.

> *The communication*
> *Of the dead is tongued with fire beyond the language of the living.*

I realize that the phrase has many meanings. There are men who die drably in the procession of events. There are others who are ennobled by 'a lifetime's death in love'. There is 'communication' made necessary 'since our concern was speech'. But this too can urge man 'to aftersight and foresight', to consecration of the past before eternity. That fire which kindles language into eloquence, is also the fire of the celestial rose, the pattern which history composes, the regeneration its humanity sustains. The words in *Little Gidding* are points of intersection.[28] They join, in the tolerance of a convening insight, the worlds

[28]'The music of a word is, so to speak, at a point of intersection: it arises from its relation first to the words immediately preceding and following it, and indefinitely to the rest of its context; and from another relation, that of its immediate meaning in that context to all the other meanings which it has had in other contexts, to its greater or less wealth of association' (*The Music of Poetry*, p. 19).

which in common experience are divided and distinguished. Always they bring us back to what is known, but it is the familiar made different by exploration, the 'intimate yet unidentifiable', the everyday alchemized into abiding strangeness.

> See, now they vanish,
> The faces and places, with the self which, as it could, loved them,
> To become renewed, transfigured, in another pattern.

It is most difficult to do justice to *Little Gidding*. You have to do the impossible, to say four things at once; and if you try to say them successively you end up by saying something different. The poem is full of reverberations from its own past, caught suddenly into audacious harmonies. The dance of *East Coker* 'signifying matrimony' can 'move in measure' through the fires of purgatory, yet scintillate in the discipline of speech. The rose in the rose-garden can become the rose of history. The poetic mastery which effects these changes extends to a corresponding power over rhythm. Thus the dull momentous movement of *The Dry Salvages*

> Here the impossible union
> Of spheres of existence is actual,
> Here the past and the future
> Are conquered and reconciled

can glide into athletic grace in *Little Gidding*:

> If I think, again, of this place,
> And of people, not wholly commendable,
> Of no immediate kin or kindness,
> But some of peculiar genius,
> All touched by a common genius,
> United in the strife which divided them;

The difference between these two passages is easy to recognize and almost impossible to isolate. It is certainly not one of prosody and it cannot usefully be declared a difference of sound. What matters, of course, is not the elements themselves, but their subtle co-operation in a poetic unity, a co-operation so complex that a critical apparatus can neither define nor capture the completeness of which this fusion is the symbol. In a sense, it is the measure of the success of the poetry that it makes such a commentary tedious and irrelevant.

Of the development of *Little Gidding* there is little I need say.

The Unity of the Quartets

The keynote of the first section is its insistence on a specific time and place and a uniformity which abides behind them: 'Here and in England'; 'It would always be the same'. This insistence is needed to tie down phrases like 'never and always' and 'meeting nowhere no before and after'. Section two glances at *East Coker*—'Dust inbreathed was a house—/The wall, the wainscot and the mouse'. We think of creation lapsing into its elements and as this expansion in our scale of imagination is forced upon us the key-words 'water and fire' lead us to the seventh circle of the Inferno. The 'fiery rain' which falls here falls also on burning London. Here Mr Eliot, fire-watcher and wanderer in Hades, meets his 'familiar compound ghost' which will provide the backbone for one hundred American theses and which as far as present knowledge can tell is Dante, Mallarmé, and Arnaut Daniel put together. The ghost promises Mr Eliot a suitably grisly future, but all that he can say, however terrible, is turned into sweetness by Eliot's *terza rima*. I say *terza rima* because that is what the paragraphing suggests. In fact the basis of the passage is a regular alternation of decasyllabic and hypermetric lines with next to no substitution and light though frequent medical stopping. The section with its continual reference of immediate facts to symbols suggests 'two worlds become much like each other'. It closes by pointing to 'purgatorial fire' and the ghost having said this fades upon the 'all-clear' leaving Mr Eliot to discuss matters with his audience.

Section three begins by suggesting 'the use of memory'. 'Attachment' is to 'detachment' roughly as 'desire' is to 'love'. Memory which helps to relate the present to the past is an act not of recollection but of detachment, an 'expansion of love beyond desire'. We remember section one—'what the dead had no speech for, when living,/They can tell you, being dead'. But from this it does not follow that we are to celebrate 'dead men more than the dying'. This is merely to 'ring the bell backwards', to harass oneself with ghosts, to surrender one's judgement to 'the spectre of a rose'. The past to be understood must be neither despised nor idolized. It is defined not by referring it to the present or the future but by referring all three to the pattern they jointly compose. One is grateful to Mr Eliot for his handling of the Civil War. It is only too easy, in discussing it, to be partisan; and it is difficult not to be partisan without appearing indifferent or obtuse. Mr Eliot does neither, and there is real understanding behind his conclusion that King Charles and Laud, Milton and Strafford lived for the same truth and died for the same finality. The poetry which soothes these acrimonies is staccato, precise yet miraculously relaxed, surging at last into joyous consecration.

> And all shall be well and
> All manner of thing shall be well
> By the purification of the motive
> In the ground of our beseeching.

Of the tremendous rhymed lyric of section four there is nothing I can say which would not be redundant. People to whom it is not immediately impressive are unlikely to be convinced by a description of its subtleties. Section five opens with a reminiscence of *East Coker*—'to make an end is to make a beginning'[29]—which leads to a memorable passage on poetic craftsmanship. I have already suggested some of the functions of this passage, but it is worth pointing out also that 'the complete consort dancing together' alludes specifically to the quotation in *East Coker* from *The Gouernor*:

> In daunsinge, signifying matrimonie—
> A dignified and commodious sacrament
> Two and two, necessarye coniunction,
> Holding eche other by the hand or the arm
> Whiche betokeneth concorde.

But in *Little Gidding* the conception does not strain against the context. The dance is not a gesture, an automatic acknowledgement of the past, but a symbol of unity between the past and the present, 'an easy commerce of the old and new'. This kind of recapitulation is important because it provides a poetic basis for a theory of tradition which might otherwise degenerate into dogma. Thus when Mr Eliot continues

> Every phrase and every sentence is an end and a beginning,
> Every poem an epitaph. And any action
> Is a step to the block, to the fire, down the sea's throat
> Or to an illegible stone: and that is where we start.

we need to recognize that the triumphant power of this statement is founded irrevocably on its poetic past. The block and

[29]See Donne's exegesis: *Complete Poetry and Selected Prose*, ed. John Hayward (London, 1929), pp. 734-5.

the fire are from *Little Gidding*. The sea's throat is from *The Dry Salvages*. The illegible stone refers us to *East Coker*: 'And not the lifetime of one man only/But of old stones that cannot be deciphered'. Thus the movement set up by the poetry itself makes it inevitable that the end should be the beginning. When we see this it is both beautiful and just that the last surge and aspiration of the poetry should take us back to the phrase which initiates *Burnt Norton*:

> *A people without history*
> *Is not redeemed from time, for history is a pattern*
> *Of timeless moments.*

And as the poetry ebbs from this magnificence, we wander back through the gate to the rose garden, and all that we have discovered in strange countries can only corroborate what we have always known.

It is customary to close an essay of more than two thousand words on Mr Eliot with a cautious prophecy that he will be among the English poets after his death. Without being reckless I should like to be more lavish. When one reads the various reviews of the Quartets the bewilderment and sheer misunderstanding with which they have often been greeted should convince us that they are radically new. Yet they are not great poems because there is nothing else in English literature like them. They are not even great because of their splendid craftsmanship. They are great because of a quality which I can only describe as utter and relentless fidelity to the event. Twenty-nine years ago Mr Eliot wrote as follows:

> . . . the historical sense involves a perception, not only of the pastness of the past but of its presence; the historical sense compels a man to write not merely with his own generation in his bones, but with a feeling that the whole of the literature of Europe from Homer and within it the whole of the literature of his own country has a simultaneous presence and composes a simultaneous order.[30]

That 'order' is the 'pattern' of the Quartets. Years of thought and of the translation of thought into poetry have intervened to make possible its now complete embodiment. Yet a single intelligence speaks across those years. And to-day in some of the most moving poetry that English literature has known, it speaks with the precision of an ultimate sincerity.

[30] 'Tradition and the Individual Talent', *Selected Essays* (London, 1934), p. 14.

Eliot's Philosophical Themes

PHILOSOPHY MAY enter the poetic economy in more than one sense. Most simply, a poem may have for its purpose the communication of independently received or conceived ideas—ideas that could be formulated accurately enough, though perhaps less agreeably, in plain logical prose. The poem and its ideas, on that basis, are distinct essences, strategically united for some reason extrinsic to the nature of either. Lucretius is proof that this kind of poetry, or something approximating to it, can rise to magnificence. Nevertheless the Lucretian mode of composition is of ambiguous validity; it plays into the hands of the stubbornly literal interpreter, who in the interests of journalism or pedagogy regards the philosophy of a poem as equivalent to whatever trim propositions can be screened out of it. At bottom this critical misunderstanding rests on what may be called the fallacy of semantic atomism—the willingness to assume that plain open statements are sufficient for all purposes of authentic communication.

In poetry, however, plain statements are less rigid than they seem; a poetic proposition is fringed with its own irony. Its very existence is sometimes a happy accident; Eliot has testified that 'a poem, or a passage of a poem, may tend to realize itself first as a particular rhythm before it reaches expression in words'. Dionysus skips ahead of Apollo, although it is Apollo who lights the way. Rhythm and ideation, song and vision, collaborate in the poetic act; and their tension motivates—perhaps even is—the poem. To say this is but to reformulate the truism that philosophical and religious ideas are poetically interesting only so far as they are assimilated to the poetic mode of apprehension.

There are for Eliot, I should judge, two supreme modes of apprehension—poetic and religious. The poetic mode is synthetic: it works by fusion of elements; the poem *qua poem* is a particular medium 'in which impressions and experiences combine in peculiar and unexpected ways.'[31] There is impersonality here—the poet transcends the accidents of his empirical self, but not in the same way as one who is engaged in the religious mode of apprehension, whose emotion, as Eliot says of Bishop Andrewes, is 'wholly evoked by the object of contemplation to which it is adequate'.[32] The poetic Eros, born of Poverty and Plenty, pursues without ever quite triumphantly grasping the good; he is always arising from, never escaping the debris of the temporal. Mediating between two worlds he is ill at ease with a straightforward philosophy. The philosophy of a poem thus appears most happily not as a doctrinal structure but as a pattern of living themes—even though a doctrinal structure, and in Dante's case a strict one, may exist as a constant background of reference.

The primary theme which stirs Eliot's poetry into intellectual movement is the barrenness of man's contemporary spiritual estate. It assumes many imagistic forms—sand and dry rock, gashouse ugliness, sandwich-paper litter, parvenu vulgarity, prostitution, hysteria, betrayal, death and half-death; underlying all of which are the two main tokens of spiritual failure—neutrality and separation. The crowd that flows over London Bridge each morning to the drab necessities of urban employment is likened to the ruined souls whom Dante's Hell rejects—moral isolationists who could not make a choice, damned followers of a wavering banner. Dante describes them by the simile of sand—its dryness, barrenness and non-resistance to the wind. Eliot thickens the imagery by evoking in his next line another scene from the *Inferno*—the Second Circle, where lust, once so alive, has withered into a stereotype, an attitude, a dull gnawing restlessness without hope of comfort, fulfilment, or release, and where the only light—as in Blake's engraving of the scene—is an ever-dimming memory of lost joy. Paolo and Francesca, although isolated in a love that had ignored external claims, retained in their mutual sense of co-presence a certain light and beauty even in Hell. Not so the hollow men, the neurotic courtesan of *The Waste Land*, Gerontion huddled in a decayed house with his senseless scraps of memory, Prufrock with his hypochondriac

[31]'Tradition and the Individual Talent', *Selected Essays* (London, 1934), p.20.
[32]'Lancelot Andrewes', *Selected Essays*, p. 341.

Philip Wheelwright

hesitations. Separation for them is only negative, a dusty lingering death. The organic principle of that death is indicated by Freud, who, in *Beyond the Pleasure Principle*, declares that 'the ruling tendency of psychic life, perhaps of nerve life altogether, is the struggle for reduction, keeping at a constant level, or removal of the inner stimulus tension', and that this 'life-process of an individual leads, from internal causes, to the equalizing of chemical tensions: i.e., to death, while union with an individually different substance increases these tensions—so to speak introduces new vital differentia, which then have to be again lived out'. The principle is an archetypal one, applying to the conditions of intense and highly serious awareness no less than to psycho-biological levels of renewal. 'The awful daring of a moment's surrender' is thus a first though not a sufficient condition of authentic living.

But if there is death in the waste land there are perils too in the surrender that beckons toward escape. Seeking the living waters we may drown in the waters of illusion. The ambivalence of the water-symbol appears to be associated by Eliot with the aphorism of Heraclitus which he quotes on the title page of *Burnt Norton*: 'Although the Word is common to all, most people live as if they had each a private wisdom of his own'. Each individual discovers moments of bright refuge in his own hyacinth or rose garden; each follows the deception of the thrush into his own first world, never identical with the first world of another. One's first world is not a shared supernatural actuality as in Maeterlinck's *Bluebird*; it is that quality of the hauntingly familiar in experience which, although it flashes so transiently, gives significance, or the illusion of significance, to moments of everyday living.

> And the bird called, in response to
> The unheard music hidden in the shrubbery,
> And the unseen eyebeam crossed, for the roses
> Had the look of flowers that are looked at.
> There they were as our guests, accepted and accepting.

The paradoxes *unheard music* and *unseen eyebeam* are expressive. In plain prose, one has the illumined feeling that such qualities are present, but while offered through sense-experience they are in con-

98

tradiction to its more obvious aspects. Mr Leonard Unger[33] has suggested that the roses represent a throwback to our normal world, having been looked at by drooping multitudes until they have lost their freshness. I disagree. The roses are among the 'other echoes' dwelling in the garden; they are said to be our guests only because the garden is, for the moment, so inviolably ours. Their appearance of being looked at comes not from the gaze of the crowd but from the unseen eyebeam in the vibrant air. The flowers in Botticelli's *Primavera*, and in a simpler, more placid way those in da Brescia's *Madonna in the Rose Garden*, disclose something of this quality.

There is now movement in a formal pattern into the 'box circle'—the English garden design that surrounds the pool. The pool, consistently with the familiar *Waste Land* imagery, is drained and dry; it fills with water as we look, the lotus arises, the surface glitters out of heart of light, then a cloud passes and the pool is seen to be empty—recalling that moment of sharper ecstasy in the hyacinth scene of *The Waste Land*, from which the disillusionment (*Oed' und leer das Meer*) was correspondingly more abrupt. Here at least we have, or seem to have, a companion and protector.

> Go, said the bird, for the leaves were full of children,
> Hidden excitedly, containing laughter.
> Go, go, go, said the bird: human kind
> Cannot bear very much reality.

Why does the bird, who just now invited us into the garden, warn us so urgently away? What is the reality of which human kind cannot bear too much? I cannot agree with Mr Unger that the garden itself is meant; that, while it lasts, is not reality but nostalgic illusion, and is very easily borne. Why am I chilled with quick fear at the laughter of children among the leaves? Is it because they, too, are about to vanish like the water of the pool? Or worse, might they in another moment suffer one of those nightmare transformations so recurrent in Eliot's poetry? What if the leaves should turn out to be the limp leaves of the Himavant jungle crouching and humped in silence?

Such metamorphoses and threats of metamorphosis find their epitomization and abstract symbol in that other Heraclitean

[33]Leonard Unger, 'T. S. Eliot's Rose Garden: A Persistent Theme', *The Southern Review*, Spring 1942.

aphorism which Eliot adopts: 'The way up and the way down are one and the same'. Heraclitus, indeed, offers promising material to poets. Life teems with contradictory situations, which systematic philosophers are at pains to resolve into logical components, but which Heraclitus, like the poets, though more baldly, undertakes to describe as they actually appear to us at moments of heightened sensitivity. 'The way up' meant to Heraclitus, outwardly, the qualitative movement from rock and earth through the intermediate stages of mud, water, cloud, air, and aether, to the rarest and uppermost of all states, which is fire; 'the way down' meant the contrary movement. Both movements are in process all the time in all things that exist, hence they are said to be 'the same'. Existence thus involves unceasing tension between upward and downward pulls—toward the realm of rarity, warmth, light and toward the realm of density, cold, dark. The pull is not only observed in physical phenomena, it operates too in our souls. 'Souls delight to get wet . . . to bathe like swine in mire . . . but the best soul is like a dry beam of light'. The inner, arcane meaning of Heraclitus's *up* and *down* is thus intensely moral, and may have been connected with religious mysteries of life and death, like those celebrated at Eleusis.

The identity—more strictly the simultaneity—of up and down is epitomized at the beginning of the second section of *Burnt Norton* by the ancient symbol of the Wheel.

> *Garlic and sapphires in the mud*
> *Clot the bedded axle-tree.*

A familiar development of the theme in medieval and renaissance iconography is the Wheel of Fortune, whirling men ceaselessly upward to prosperity and downward to misery. But always at the centre of the Wheel's movement, conditioning it, is the axle-tree. Although the visible axle-tree evidently turns, for it is an empirical part of the wheel, there is an axis at the centre of the axle-tree, a mathematically pure point, which remains unmoving —'the still point of the turning world'—and which 'reconciles' the contradictions of the surrounding movement. The perfect axle, therefore, symbolizes the ultimate point of human aspiration; garlic and sapphires, the two usual kinds of impediment to its attainment. Garlic has symbolic affinities with some of the less lovely images of Eliot's earlier poems—'the damp souls of housemaids', Gerontion's dull head among windy spaces, Apeneck Sweeney erect, the rat with slimy belly, Mr Eugenides, the young man carbuncular, the 'winter evening round behind the gashouse', the cactus land, 'the toothed gullet of an aged shark'. Sapphires symbolize, I judge, whatever is deceptively lovely in experience; and are reminiscent, therefore, of such earlier symbols as Princess Volupine, *la figlia che piange*, Belladonna Lady of the Rocks, the jewels of the modern Cleopatra and the eyes turned into pearls, Elizabeth and Leicester beating oars on the not yet sullied Thames, the silken girls bringing sherbet, and the many other scenes and references suggesting promise that exceeds the possibility of fulfilment. Sapphires and garlic thus reinforce the up-down movement of the wheel and of the imagery in the fifteen-line stanza in which they occur.

But all this errs by over-simplifying; the Heraclitean paradox must be qualified. The way up and the way down, while the same, are yet not the same. For sapphires suggest also the blue rocks of *Ash Wednesday*, St Simeon's Roman hyacinths blooming in bowls, and in the present poem the experience of the rose garden—symbols not utterly deceptive, for their promise is indeed real if only we undertake the required self-discipline and do not expect fulfilment in terms of the temporally actual, i.e., of rewards. 'The trilling wire in the blood'—an electrical metaphor that recalls also the bird's song—is the physiological correlative of the rose-garden experience; for although it is a disturbing factor and the cause of illusions, its promptings induce moments of insight into the world's moving pattern, whence we can

> . . . *hear upon the sodden floor*
> *Below, the boarhound and the boar*
> *Pursue their pattern as before*
> *But reconciled among the stars.*

In addition to their pictorial evocation of the tapestry of the hunt, the boarhound and boar, alluding no doubt to the myth of Tammuz or Adonis (cf. Floret in *Animula*), symbolize the rhythm of desire and death, of summer and winter.

The locale of *The Dry Salvages* permits a more positive presentation of the water symbol than that furnished by the drowned Phœnician sailor of *The Waste Land*. Other symbols are brought into connection with the sea: the river, the rock, the tolling bell, the wreckage on the river and on the beach, and—as always—time. Mr Unger, in the article already cited, suggests that the ocean, river and rocks are symbolic expressions of what Eliot calls 'the primitive terror', in that while seeming to be controlled by secular civilization, they continue actually as menacing and destructive; and of the sea he adds: 'In its immense shapelessness it represents history as other than "sequence" and "development" '. So far I am in agreement; the sea has symbolic affinity with history's cunning corridors in *Gerontion*, with the stylistic discontinuities of *The Waste Land* explicated and resolved in 'These fragments I have shored against my ruins', and with the paradoxes at the beginning of *Burnt Norton*. Its time, other than the time of clocks and calendars, is measured by the tolling bell, rung by the unhurried ground swell. It is a time 'between midnight and dawn, when the past is all deception,/The future futureless'—not ordered into a linear progress but catching us unawares in moments of sudden illumination.

Now into the sea flows the river, 'a strong brown god— sullen, untamed and intractable/. . . . Unhonoured, unpropitiated/By worshippers of the machine, but waiting, watching and waiting'. What does the river symbolize beyond that primitive terror, that Sense of the Abyss, as Dr Tillich calls it, which permeates all the major symbols of the poem? I take it to be a near-equivalent of 'the trilling wire in the blood' in *Burnt Norton* and of 'the fever sings in mental wires' in *East Coker*; what I have called the physiological correlative of the moment of illumined experience; the pulse-beat by which we respond to the hyacinth ecstasy, to the laughter in the garden, and now to 'the sea howl and the sea yelp'. For it is stated that 'the river is within us, the sea is all about us'. And wreckage clutters them both. The sea tosses up to shore 'its hints of earlier and other creation:/The starfish, the hermit crab, the whale's backbone'. Our losses too it tosses up—shattered lobster-pots, broken oars, and the gear of foreign dead men. And the river likewise is choked 'with its cargo of dead Negroes, cows and chicken coops'. No purity here —'no end to the withering of withered flowers'. But time that destroys also preserves; every detail of the pattern is ambivalent; even Adam's lust is seen in contrary perspectives, as 'the bitter apple and the bite in the apple'. And as a special symbol of permanence in the midst of change there is 'the ragged rock in the restless waters', washed by waves, concealed by fogs, a monument on halcyon days, a sea-mark in navigable weather, 'but in the sombre season/Or the sudden fury, is what it always was'. Whether by intention or accident this last phrase translates literally Aristotle's idiom for unchanging essence, *to ti en einai*.

The rock is what it always was; the water surrounding it has the contrary kind of immortality—its eternity is of process rather than of being. That ineluctable antithesis, Being and Becoming, is thus vividly hypostatized. But the hypostasis is not static, nor is it defined by the strategies of traditional metaphysics. For as both rock and water are ambivalent symbols, by what token shall their positive meanings be distinguished from their negative? The answer is supplied in another dimension from the abstractly cognitive. It is the redeeming Lady of Silences who in *Ash Wednesday* 'made cool the dry rock and made firm the sand'. It is in her presence that 'the fountain sprang up' —no longer a mirage or a drowning flood—and 'the bird sang down'—not now deceptive. She is at once the 'blessed sister holy mother' and also the 'spirit of the fountain, spirit of the garden'. But she stands between the yews (Eliot's familiar death symbol), a little remote from casual apprehension, with bent head and silent. To approach her requires a surmounting discipline of the stair, or ladder, of purgative contemplation—a discipline for the expression of which Dante and St John of the Cross furnish abundant imagery.

The mention of Krishna in Part III of *The Dry Salvages* makes explicit the strain of Eastern philosophy adumbrated in *The Waste Land* and elsewhere in the *Four Quartets*. The doctrine of Sankhya Yoga which Krishna embodied as charioteer expounds to the young Prince Arjuna in the *Bhagavad-gita* contains not only ideas but also specific symbols used by Eliot. The darkness symbol:

> In that which is night to all things, therein the self-subjugated remains awake; but where all else is awake, that is night for the knower of the self.[34]

[34]II, 69. Adapted from Swami Parmananda's translation.

Philip Wheelwright

Contending phases of the sea symbol:

> The mind that yields to the uncontrolled and wandering senses lets its wisdom float adrift as a boat on water is borne away by the wind.[35]

And

> As the ocean remains calm and unaltered though the waters flow into it, so a self-controlled saint remains unmoved when desires enter into him.[36]

Certain of Krishna's teachings about the nature of the transition called death are used by Eliot with striking subtlety. Krishna's words are these:

> He who, at the time of death, thinking of Me alone, goes forth, leaving the body, he attains unto My being. Have no doubt of this.

> O son of Kunti, whatever state of being one dwells upon in the end, at the time of leaving the body, that alone he attains because of his constant thought of that state of being. . . .

> The majority of beings, coming into birth again and again, merge helplessly into the unmanifested at the approach of night and become manifest at the approach of day.

> But beyond this unmanifested there is another Unmanifested which is eternally existent and is not destroyed even when all things are destroyed.[37]

Eliot's restatement, which at one point becomes literal translation, may be compared:

> *At the moment which is not of action or inaction*
> *You can receive this: 'on whatever sphere of being*
> *The mind of a man may be intent*
> *At the time of death'—that is the one action*
> *(And the time of death is every moment)*
> *Which shall fructify in the lives of others:*
> *And do not think of the fruit of action.*
> *Fare forward.*

In Eliot's version the emphasis shifts away from the Hindu idea of a sequence of definite incarnations determined by the law of Karma; the parenthesized qualification is a reminder of the Heraclitean remark that 'you cannot step twice into the same river, for other and yet other waters are ever flowing on'. Each moment is a dying and therefore (since time is never finished)

[35] *Ibid.*, II, 67. Adapted from Swami Parmananda's translation.

[36] *Ibid.*, II, 70. Here I take it is a secondary grace-note meaning of Eliot's symbol.

[37] *Ibid.*, VIII, 5-6, 19-20.

always in some sense a rebirth. 'Fire lives in the death of air, and air in the death of fire; water lives in the death of earth, and earth in the death of water'. Life and death to Heraclitus's vision are opposite but logically inextricable sides of every phenomenon, like up and down, convex and concave. But life and rebirth in this primitive sense have no distinctive reference to the human spirit. They describe simply the brute fact of temporal existence. What matters is the *quality* of rebirth, the degree to which one 'attains unto My being' as Krishna has said. Eliot's sure catalytic instinct here, furnishing the main philosophical theme of the poem, has been to synthesize the Hindu idea of rebirth through self-disciplined and reverent concentration upon 'the Unmanifested beyond the unmanifested' (i.e., the Dark that is sought by the devoted soul, not merely the darkness of the weary round of time) with Heraclitus's idea of the relevance of rebirth to every temporal moment. Since the future like the past is an imaginative construction and only the present is actual, an incessantly moving *now*, rebirth must be an experience of the *now*—not a future hope but a present embarkation, a resolute 'faring forward'.

But seafaring is not to be undertaken lightly: remember the watery death of Phlebas the Phœnician. Corresponding to the defunctive music of that episode in *The Waste Land*, there is in *The Dry Salvages* a mariner's prayer:

> *Lady, whose shrine stands on the promontory,*
> *Pray for all those who are in ships, those*
> *Whose business has to do with fish. . . .*

This is again she who 'walked between the violet and the violet' —at once the *figlia del tuo figlio*, Queen of Heaven, and one's earthly intercessor and means of salvation, found wherever the spirit can know and choose her. The fisher symbol stirs memories of the wounded Fisher King (identified in the Grail legend with the divine principle of life and fertility), the public bar 'where fishmen lounge at noon', neighbouring the almost hidden white and gold splendour of the Church of St Magnus Martyr, and—as probably in all Eliot's uses of this symbol—Matthew iv, 19. One's resolution must be unstinted—'a condition of complete simplicity/(Costing not less than everything)', in the words of *Little Gidding*. Let there be, as Krishna taught, right action, independent of 'fruits' and freed thereby of servitude to past and future. An unrealizable aim for inhabitants of this twittering world, but its unrealizability does not imply total defeat.

> We, content at the last
> If our temporal reversion nourish
> (Not too far from the yew-tree)
> The life of significant soil.

The yew-tree is always nearby. We cannot, nor will any theology, Hindu or Christian, persuade us that we can uproot it. But our one known task remains: to cultivate and set in order the lands on which it grows.

A Question of Speech

You don't speak soundly and agreeably, you don't speak neatly and consistently, unless you *know* how you speak . . . and you have not this positive consciousness, you are incapable of any reaction of taste or sensibility worth mentioning, unless a great deal of thought of the matter has been taken *for* you.

HENRY JAMES: *The Question of our Speech*

In the present age the poet—(I would wish to be understood as speaking generally, and without allusion to individual names)— seems to propose to himself as his main object, and as that which is most characteristic of his art, new and striking images; with incidents that interest the affections or excite the curiosity . . . . In his diction and metre, on the other hand, he is comparatively careless. The measure is either constructed on no previous system, and acknowledges no justifying principle but that of the writer's convenience; or else some mechanical movement is adopted, of which one couplet or stanza is so far an adequate specimen, as that the occasional differences appear evidently to arise from accident, or the qualities of the language itself, not from meditation and an intelligent purpose.

S. T. COLERIDGE: *Biographia Literaria*

POETS AND poetasters can be very much alike in their experience of reading and writing poetry, so my observation tells me, and therefore it does not much matter to which category one belongs, for the purpose of generalizing from one's own experience. I must make this point to begin with, because when someone of either category writes 'the contemporary poet' he is apt to think first of himself; and when he writes of a living master, he is apt to think first of his own debt. I propose to concern myself with the debt which any poet writing now, and other poets to come, must owe to T. S.

Eliot, rather than with the movement of literary fashions, or his influence on any particular poets. Are his standards the ones which poetry must always keep in sight, however it may circle as a train climbs round a tower in mountains? And is the particular emphasis which he has given the most useful one for our time? Is he the writer to whom young poets have chiefly turned for help in finding their own voices?

This last service, vital as it may be to the young poet in search of a style, is not the most important that a writer can do for his contemporaries—at any rate, it can be given by small poets as well as, or even better than, by great ones, and the more immature the poet, the easier it is to learn from him, or from amateurs like the Elizabethan Robert Hayman or the twentieth-century Edward Thomas. As W. H. Auden has put it, 'The young can learn best from those of whom, because they can criticize them, they are not afraid'.[38] Eliot's development was too complete at every stage, he worked his quarries (with the exception of the drama) too thoroughly, for him to be a convenient model. True, he has had a host of imitators, but their gains seem ill-gotten, their feathers remain obviously borrowed feathers. Impossible not to be aware of poetical gawkiness, by the side of so graceful, conscious and mature a writer. Wyndham Lewis puts it with characteristic vigour in *Men Without Art*:

> This mandarin, certainly, has succeeded in instilling a salutary *fear of speech—a terror of the word*, into his youthful followers: they have not thought twice, but a dozen times or more, before committing themselves to paper, and when they have come to do so, have spoken, 'neither loud (n)or long'. They may not always have had much to say but they have said it in the fewest possible words. Indeed the mere act of writing (I have heard some of their confessions) has been undertaken with as much trepidation as the Victorian young man experienced in 'popping the question'.

Moreover, although to learn to be a poet is to learn the art of pillaging, Eliot's and Pound's method of direct quotation is apt to be a disastrous one in other hands, as Ronald Bottrall's first book of poems shows; Auden pointed to a more adaptable way[39]. I. A. Richard's suggestion that quotation performs a work of

[38]'On Hardy': *Purpose*, July-December 1940.

[39]For example, 'O where are you going? said reader to rider' in *The Orators*, the 'early English' passages in *Paid on Both Sides*; and the modern ballads.

concentration in *The Waste Land*, a poem which he says would otherwise have needed to be of epic length, is an attractive one, but I doubt whether it is true. At any rate, this seems a purely personal technique, liable to degenerate in other hands into mere patchwork.

It is, I am convinced, the perfection of his form at every stage that has caused imitations of Eliot to remain imitations merely, rather than the fact that the form was too fluid to be adapted to any other purpose than Eliot's own—which is the reason advanced by Stephen Spender in his analysis of *Prufrock*,[40] where he says that 'architecture has been sacrificed to music'. Spenser's stanza and Pope's heroic couplet were architectural enough for any purpose, but these two masters none the less used up their possibilities, and imitation of their forms, as of Eliot's, always tends to deteriorate into travesty.

For the generations following Eliot, then, it was a more voluble poet who loosened their tongues and helped them to be at ease (perhaps in the case of some, less gifted than their model, even too much at ease) with their subject-matter. It was Auden's use of stanza and stress which proved the easier for the novice to handle: the strict stanza form to contain his inchoate ideas (for 'Free verse is only to be used by those in whom the intention and the power are one')[41] and the governance of stress and alliteration, adapted from the early English forms, to give him freedom within the line (used also by Eliot in his dramatic verse). For myself, I should say that it was Eliot who first made me despair of becoming a poet; Auden (with, of course, dead poets, notably Sir Thomas Wyatt) who first made me think I saw how to become one. Both services are equally necessary. But when the start has once been made, what else will the young writer look for, and find, in Eliot's work?

A prime question for poetry now, as it is for mankind, is the question of self-consciousness. Is it possible to be too much aware of what one is and of what one does? Science and philosophy must, by their very nature, return a negative to that question; but religion and poetry? We need not answer here for religion, though the discipline of the mystics and the rituals of the Church alike tend to keep the dark places dark, while un-

[40] *The Destructive Element.*

[41] Auden, *op. cit.*

known desires are satisfied. But the life-blood of poetry is symbolism, and symbols are essentially *hiding places* of power. The poet will do his work better if he has his conscious mind occupied with technical problems, rather than with the libidinous origin of his subject-matter; and the same process will then operate in his readers. Poetry must always be a feeding-cup for ideas, making its readers, for the instant, greater than they are. Now Eliot's example can be supremely valuable here, for in his critical writings, and on the whole in his poetry, he has turned not so much towards an increased self-consciousness as towards a keener consciousness of method and choice of form: considering 'not merely "what am I to say?" but rather "how and to whom am I to say it?" '[42] And while Auden is so much of a virtuoso that he can turn almost any model to good account, Eliot's method is more selective: his achievement has been to find out precisely what he can do, and never to allow the question of what he cannot, to arise in the reader's mind.

I think that Eliot's preoccupation with the personal and impersonal in art is directly related to this problem of self-consciousness, and that what may seem to be a contradiction between his early and late opinions (see his Yeats Memorial Lecture[43]) is resolved if you look at it so. For it is the wrong kind of self-consciousness, which is vividly aware only of its own emotions, and is possessed by the wish to communicate an emotion rather than by the wish to write a poem, that results in what Henry James called 'the terrible *fluidity* of self-revelation'[44] —always anathema to T. S. Eliot. The hero of *Portrait of a Lady* may have felt disgust with the method:

> And I must borrow every changing shape
> To find expression, dance dance
> Like a dancing bear
> Cry like a parrot, chatter like an ape

but then the young man in that poem is (as his creator remarked of Hamlet) unable to find the true definition of his emotion: his *personae* are inadequate. T. S. Eliot is, it is true, a dramatic poet, but whether lyric or dramatic makes little difference in this context, for in either it is a question of emotion personal in origin,

[42] *The Use of Poetry and the Use of Criticism* (London, 1934).

[43] *Purpose*, July-December 1940.

[44] Preface to *The Ambassadors*.

but in expression, typical. 'We all have to choose whatever subject-matter affords us the deepest and most secret release'.[45]

T. S. Eliot said of Matthew Arnold that in his criticism he sometimes chose *personae*, or masks, behind which he could go through his own performance, and that 'sometimes a critic may choose an author to criticize, a role to assume, as far as possible the antithesis to himself, a personality which has actualized all that has been suppressed in himself; we can sometimes arrive at a very satisfactory intimacy with our anti-masks'[46]—which is interesting in connexion with Eliot's own work. But he also said 'One feels that the writing of poetry brought him (i.e., Arnold) little of that excitement, that joyful loss of self in the workmanship of art, that intense and transitory relief which comes at the moment of completion and is the chief reward of creative work'. That is the right place for the conscious will: as Coleridge put it, 'an interpenetration of passion and of will, of *spontaneous* impulse and of *voluntary* purpose'.[47]

Take next 'the question of our speech'. In considering a new movement in the arts, you may speak of revolution or rediscovery: probably, at this stage in history, the second word will always be the more accurate, though the critic who referred to Ezra Pound and T. S. Eliot as 'drunken helots' would probably have preferred the former. The battle may be one that has been fought two or three times before in our own literary history, and lately fought and won across the Channel—as is this battle of the colloquial idiom—but the point is that if poetry is to continue to live, there must be a battle, and poets of sufficient stature to open it. The badness of bad poetry may not vary very much—if you open *The Oxford Book of English Verse* at random among the 'moderns' and read

> But the floods and the tears meet and gather;
> The sound of them all grows like thunder:
> —O into what bosom, I wonder,
> Is pour'd the whole sorrow of years?
>> For Eternity only seems keeping
>> Account of the great human weeping:
>> May God, then, the Maker and Father—
>> May He find a place for the tears!

[45]T. S. Eliot, *Selected Poems by Marianne Moore* (London, 1935), Intro., p. 9.
[46]*The Use of Poetry and the Use of Criticism*, p. 108.
[47]*Biographia Literaria*, ed. J. Shawcross (London, 1907), Vol. II, p. 50.

Anne Ridler

then Tambimuttu's *Poetry in Wartime* and read

> It is not too late though the clocks of Europe cull
> Their separate times,
> And blood and lies skew nations like teetotums,
> It is not too late for the resilience of existence,
> Forgiveness may still look out of the slits of eyes.

you may think that there is not much to choose between them; but it is in the genuine but minor talents that the benefits of a tradition show, and I think that our minor poets are better than those of the late nineteenth-century—'you are incapable of any reaction of taste and sensibility . . . unless a great deal of thought of the matter has been taken *for* you'. An age can afford a few good poets who stand aside from this battle for the colloquial idiom in poetry, and continue to use the artificial diction of an earlier generation—as, in our own day, are such diverse poets as Walter de la Mare and Charles Williams—but not many; and with these, the young must 'admire and do otherwise', as Hopkins put it. It can also afford a different kind of poet, who treats words as though he were present at their creation—a Dylan Thomas or a George Barker—but only if the main channel is kept clear. These are the luxury of a strong tradition: they effect a renewal of words, but it is as transient as the result of a dose of benzedrine on a human being; a pick-me-up like the nonsense-writing of Edward Lear—though I do not mean to belittle the startling refreshment of words which you find, for instance, in this sentence from the story of Guy, Violet, Lionel and Slingsby: 'They went on their way with the utmost delight and apathy'. Here the renewal is contrived by forgetting the practical sense of the word, or rather by going back to the sense it had when, in childhood, it was something composed of sound, the shape of syllables seen on the printed page, and the form of the mouth that spoke them. But when T. S. Eliot revives or coins a word (and 'revives' has two meanings here), it is always by a close attention to the sense and derivation. There are many examples, from 'demotic' in *The Waste Land* and 'dissembled' in *Ash Wednesday*,[48] to 'prevents us everywhere' in *East Coker* and 'significant soil' in *The Dry Salvages*.[49] And the careful juxtaposition is every-

---

[48] 'I who am here dissembled'—a coining of meaning which keeps in mind the origin of the word.

[49] In James Joyce, of course, you find both these kinds of renewal.

thing, to make the word the right one:

> *The word neither diffident nor ostentatious,*
> *An easy commerce of the old and the new,*
> *The common word exact without vulgarity,*
> *The formal word precise but not pedantic,*
> *The complete consort dancing together.*[50]

'Living, the poet is carrying on that struggle for the maintenance of a living language, for the maintenance of its strength, its subtlety, for the preservation of quality of feeling, which must be kept up in every generation; dead, he provides standards for those who take up the struggle after him'[51]: there is T. S. Eliot's conception of the poet's function, and nowhere has it been more to the point than in the drama. We owe it to W. B. Yeats and to Eliot that it is possible to attempt poetic drama again, although we are still far from having a tradition secure enough to lift the burden of perpetual choice of style from the poet's shoulders: a tradition in which he can deal with any kind of subject-matter without having recourse to prose. Auden's use of prose for drama—for instance in *The Ascent of F6* and in his Christmas Oratorio—is I think more successful than Eliot's, more of a piece with his poetic style than the Shavian dialogue of the Knights in *Murder in the Cathedral*, though his plays as a whole remain a hotch-potch, brilliant experiments only. But Eliot achieved a style which could do without prose in *The Family Reunion*, and it is in that direction that playwrights will have to follow. For Yeats's plays achieve unity by their brevity: a single mood is maintained at a high pitch of intensity throughout, so that the question of a change of style does not arise. Moreover, in Ireland there was a speech of peasants already near to poetry; in England this speech was more nearly lost, and the gap between common talk and verse was harder to bridge: poetry had to come further towards prose, and sometimes became self-conscious in the process—for instance, in those moments in *Murder in the Cathedral* when Eliot seems to be parodying himself:

I see nothing quite conclusive in the art of temporal government,

or

You are right to express a certain incredulity.

It may be that later on we shall see a reaction, so that Beddoes

[50]*Little Gidding.*
[51]*Selected Poems by Marianne Moore*, Intro., p. 6.

will become as popular as Crabbe is now; but at present the problem is to discover (as Eliot has formulated it) how people of the present day would talk, if they could talk poetry; and we are at least clear about what has to be done.

For the Symbolists, poetry was an art that 'should not inform but suggest and evoke, not name things but create their atmosphere',[52] so that, as Mallarmé said, 'la Musique rejoint le Vers pour former, depuis Wagner, la Poésie'; while for T. E. Hulme's 'hard, dry, classical verse', the 'great aim is accurate, precise and definite description'.[53] Both these strains meet in Eliot's verse, and it is only for theorists that a poet must belong exclusively to one or the other category, and a painter to one or the other of the now-fashionable categories, of those who look to the reality behind externals, and those who are content to set down the evidence of their eyes. With the second type of verse in mind, you may set beside Gautier's *L'Art*

> *Peintre, fuis l'aquarelle,*
> *Et fixe la couleur*
> > *Trop frêle*
> *Au four de l'émailleur.*

> . . . . . .

> *Dans son nimbe trilobe*
> *La Vierge et son Jésus,*
> > *Le globe*
> *Avec la croix dessus.*

these stanzas from *Mr Eliot's Sunday Morning Service*:

> *A painter of the Umbrian school*
> *Designed upon a gesso ground*
> *The nimbus of the Baptized God.*
> *The wilderness is cracked and browned*

> *But through the water pale and thin*
> *Still shine the unoffending feet*
> *And there above the painter set*
> *The Father and the Paraclete.*

It is chiefly, I suppose, on the question of music, that Eliot comes near to Mallarmé's point of view (and Mallarmé has his

[52]C. M. Bowra, *The Heritage of Symbolism* (London, 1943) from which I also take the quotation from Mallarmé.

[53]*Speculations*, ed. Herbert Read (London, 1936), p. 132 *et passim*.

part in the 'familiar compound ghost' of *Little Gidding*). Parallels between the two arts have always interested him: he has adopted the terminology of music, and has experimented with the use of its forms for poetry. I suspect that in order to be able to make use of the comparison, you need either to know only a little about music, or else to hold what you know in abeyance, since it requires as much subordination of the nature of music to that of poetry, as the musician necessarily makes of poetry when he sets words to melody (as distinct from recitative). Far back at the source, the similarities may be close (as Eliot has said that he feels a rhythm before thinking of any words), but as soon as the creation of form is reached, I think that the differences are more suggestive than the similarities. The elementary fact that poetry has no sustained notes is a big one: 'duration in time' is therefore quite a different thing for her, and she cannot mingle her themes in the way that music does. To compensate for her inability to keep several voices going at once, she has her hidden dimension of memory and association: this is the 'Invisible Knight' which is her constant companion. Then, the subtleties of poetic rhythm are produced by the variations of accent and speed in ordinary speech, and it is the poet's business to use these, not to violate them; or if the rhythm of his line goes against them, to contrive it so rarely and consciously as to produce a double possibility, that marvellous ambiguity which is one of the most complex joys of poetry. (An example of this particular effect is in the movement beginning 'Lady whose shrine stands on the promontory', in *The Dry Salvages*.) There is syncopation in music, and the overriding of bar lines such as you find in madrigals, but no ambiguity like this. Yet for metrical analysis, which can only approximate to truth, some such synthesis of duration and accent as music can provide, is undoubtedly helpful; and for hints and suggestions to the poet, beyond which Eliot is careful not to go, the comparison can be useful.[54]

In the poetry of Eliot and Yeats, their use of particular symbols in a way analogous to the use of musical themes, makes us

[54]I have read an attempt to imitate a piece of music in a poem written for five voices speaking at once, which merely imitated the Tower of Babel. Much nearer to one kind of music is a line such as Eliot's 'Stone, bronze, stone, steel, stone, oakleaves, horses' hooves' which evokes in an extraordinary way the sound and movement of horses going over paving stones.

more certain that their recurrence is deliberate than do the symbols of earlier poets.[55] But this does not mean that the original *choice* of symbol was more wholly conscious. Others have examined the symbols in Eliot's poetry, and pointed out their recurrence (some of them from first to last): water and fire; the sea and the river; the mouse in the wainscot; the speech of birds; the rose; fog; the wheel. They recur, but their significance sometimes changes. Take Eliot's own particular twilight, whether of dawn or evening. In *Prufrock*, with the 'yellow fog that rubs its back upon the window-panes', we are still with Dickens, the imagery is consciously fanciful and the twilight fashionable; in *The Waste Land* ('Unreal City . . .'), there is a Dantesque and hopeless Limbo[56]; in both *The Hollow Men* and *Ash Wednesday*, a 'dream-crossed twilight between birth and dying', though in the one poem the place is despair, and in the other, a place of waiting; while in *Little Gidding* 'in the uncertain hour before the morning', it is with Dante again, but not hopeless: merely illusionless and cold, with the kind of peace that comes from loving the Good merely because it *is* the Good, and not because it holds any beauty or solace.

'A man who is capable of experience finds himself in a different world in every decade of his life; as he sees it with different eyes, the material of his art is continually renewed'.[57] It is impossible to distinguish here between personal and poetic development, for if a man exhausts the possibilities of a form, is it not because he himself has changed from what he was when he first used it? Yet the temptation to repeat oneself, having found a successful manner, is resisted by few. With Eliot, each stage is complete in itself: the most striking quality in his poems is not their virtuosity (though he can display this) but their *finish*; in omission as well as inclusion his scrupulousness shows. I cannot offhand think of any redundant epithet in his poetry, except the 'Burn invisible and dim' of the 'Sunday Morning Service', where one epithet makes the other meaningless. You find in him

[55]Similarly the use of an *emotional* connexion of ideas, to the exclusion of the intellectual connexion, is more deliberate: in earlier poets it existed, as C. S. Lewis has pointed out in the case of Milton, but they always provided 'a facade of logical connexions' as well.

[56]Not strictly Limbo, but the place of those 'who never were alive'.

[57]Yeats Memorial Lecture.

no such spectacular change, from being one kind of poet to being another, as there was in Yeats (for the good reason that he found himself as a poet much sooner), and superficially his late method is like his earlier—he still proceeds from the grandiloquent to the ironical: strikes an attitude, and then gives a mocking or critical comment. But the purpose for which the method is used is different. In the earlier poems, one feels that it is dictated by caution; it is a way of avoiding self-committal; just as his view of human beings in the earlier poems, which is, one may agree with Wyndham Lewis, a satirical one, is sometimes too remote to be successful even as satire.[58] But in the later poems the change of mood is used to gain a dimension, to see all round the subject. 'That was a way of putting it, not very satisfactory . . .' is the poet making another attempt to approach the inexpressible, and showing the process as part of his attempt, like the famous 'false starts' in the Choral Symphony. It does not come from caution; it comes, as do the protests of inarticulacy, and the use of paradox which is allied to these, from a sense of overwhelming meaning to be conveyed.

> Words strain,
> Crack and sometimes break, under the burden,
> Under the tension, slip, slide, perish,
> Decay with imprecision, will not stay in place. . . .

The earlier view of life was on the whole a simpler one, and lent itself more easily to an epigrammatic style (which seems to be the reason why a critic such as George Orwell, and others more negligible, prefers the earlier—apart from ideological prejudice); Eliot's development has been, in prose as well as in verse, towards a greater inclusiveness. As a critic, he has kept his preferences while shedding his prejudices[59]; as a poet, he has kept his pity and shed his contempt for mankind.

If the influence of Eliot is less obvious than it was some fifteen years ago, when Edmund Wilson published *Axel's Castle* and rat's

[58] E.g., 'I am aware of the damp souls of housemaids', etc. Do I find this cheap because of a snobbish feeling that housemaids are not fair game? I think it is rather because the poet has not sufficiently proved the connexion between *damp* and their souls, as a class.

[59] Compare his early essay on 'The Function of Criticism' with the much less acid *What is a Classic?*; his early remarks on Milton with those in *The Music of Poetry*; and his rather grudging praise of Yeats in *After Strange Gods*, with his later Yeats Memorial Lecture.

feet and broken glass were all the rage, that does not mean that it is less pervasive. If younger poets have become impatient of such an exacting master, and write essays to prove their independence, that does but prove that they feel the pull. And it is of something deeper than the borrowing of imagery that I have tried to write. For above all, Eliot provides the necessary standard of perfection: something at once impossible and always within our grasp, the 'something evermore about to be'. This line is tinged with an irony for us, which Wordsworth certainly did not intend, but Eliot's poetry can afford and transcend the irony; it is why our debt to him is immense.

Eliot's Critical Method

HOWEVER THE arbitrament of general principles may uphold the dignity of letters, it is by the example of his practice that a critic educates his public. Mr Eliot has inflexibly supported the autonomy, if not always, the impersonality, of poetry: but when the literary history of the last twenty-five years comes to be written—although it is almost the prerogative of such histories to mention everything and to deal with nothing—the influence of Mr Eliot as a critic must surely be noted rather in the history of taste than in the history of ideas. Stress would fall on the revalution of particular writers—Marlowe, Jonson, Donne, Marvell, Massinger, Dryden—which is not so much Mr Eliot's achievement as what he has enabled this generation to achieve for itself. He gave us the tools, and those who grew up in the second half of the nineteen-twenties find it very difficult to make an impersonal assessment of the value of his method. For it was as examples of critical method that *Homage to John Dryden* (1924) and *The Sacred Wood* (1920) were canonized in the Cambridge of the time; and though Mr Eliot may be relieved that the incense no longer fumes upon local altars with quite its old intensity, he has not suffered that abrupt descent from the pedestal decreed to other idols of those days.

While he has subsequently written at greater length, and far more widely, I think that Mr Eliot's most valuable critical work is contained in the two little books I have mentioned, together with the essay on *Dante* (1929); that is to say, roughly in the first five sections of his *Selected Essays* (1932).[60] A few other essays should be added: in particular the preface to Samuel Johnson's

[60]For the reader's convenience, my subsequent references will be to this volume (cited as *S. E.*) where possible. It does not contain all the Essays from *The Sacred Wood*.

London and *The Vanity of Human Wishes*, in the Haslewood Books (1930). I shall confine myself to these works because they are the seminal and therefore the abiding portions of his critical writing. Critical journalism, lectures, and propaganda for literature have their function, but the more completely they fulfil it, the less likely they are to survive except as buoyed up by a general reputation.

In the works I have mentioned, Eliot quite dazzlingly set the fashion for the times. Donne and the metaphysicals had always been an acquired taste of the scholar; they were appreciated by some in the older universities; but it is thanks to Mr Eliot that every Higher Certificate examiner may now count infallibly upon a reference of astonished rapture to the similes of the compasses in *A Valediction*: *forbidding Mourning*, and of the map in *A Valediction*: *of Weeping*.[61] I was recently informed that beds and cartography were the outstanding interests in Donne's life. In *The Sacred Wood*, Mr Eliot could refer to Tournour's lines

> Doth the silkworm expend her yellow labours . . .

as 'unfamiliar'.[62] By now they are probably among the most frequently cited lines of Jacobean verse.

The taste of the twenties and the early thirties was for the analytic, the complicated—as distinct from the complex—and the idiosyncratic in literature. If you were subtle, you had to deploy your subtlety. If you were not subtle ('mature', 'adjusted', 'aware' were variant terms) you were damned. Dr Richard's quantitative theory of poetic value[63] was symptomatic.

Naturally Donne, the metaphysicals and the 'Shakespeareans' among Jacobean dramatists fitted in with such a mood. The new interest in Ben Jonson and Dryden perhaps represented more of a personal triumph for Mr Eliot. But 'poetry of the surface'—and how subtle to be able to recognize and subsist upon the surface!—had its attractions for a generation whose hunger for wit and fear of metaphysics were equally soothed by the 'meta-

[61] Is it too much to hope that Professor F. P. Wilson has silenced part of this deafening chorus? (*Elizabethan and Jacobean*, p. 30).

[62] In 'Tradition and the Individual Talent' (*S. E.*, p. 20).

[63] 'The purpose of the theory is just to enable us to compare different experiences in terms of their value; and their value, I suggest, is a quantitative matter. To put it briefly, the best life is that in which as much as possible of our possible personality is engaged' (*Principles of Literary Criticism*, 2nd ed., 1926, p. 288).

physical' poets. The subject of 'Poetry and Belief' was much discussed at the time—Mr Eliot made his own contribution[64] and though Mr Wisdom was not yet constituted Wittgenstein's John the Baptist, the 'Blue Book' and other stolen and surreptitious copies of the master's lectures were circulated under the counter.

As the nineteen-thirties drew on, the fashion for Donne gradually went out. Mr Eliot, in an article on Dante and Donne, which appeared only in French, showed the way the wind blew. His essay on *Dante* has been followed not only by considerable general interest in Dante, but by a cult of the later Middle Ages which threatens to become as monotonously vociferous as the cult of the metaphysical poets.

It may be summed up in the slogan 'The Renaissance didn't happen'. Medieval habits of reasoning, the medieval cosmography, the hierarchic principle, the doctrine of humours, the fourfold system of literary interpretation, the schemes of rhetoric and the allegoric mode have suddenly been grasped by the general mind: they are no longer quaint or primitive or mechanical: their survival is eagerly charted in Shakespeare, Jonson, the Elizabethan dramatists, the Elizabethan sonneteers and before long no doubt will be canvassed in Bacon. Of course Mr Eliot is not singly responsible for this fashion. Many works of scholarship have contributed to it and many influences outside the literary field. But the essay on Dante is one of the first signs of the new movement in England: Mr Eliot proved himself here at the growing point of his generation, whilst in his earlier work he had recovered the seventeenth-century traditions and 'revived old communications',[65] not only for the common reader, but also for younger writers, who have learned almost as much from Eliot's criticism as from his verse.[66]

When *The Sacred Wood* and *Homage to John Dryden* appeared, Mr Eliot was still the subject of frightened abuse in the weeklies, and also in some academic circles. But his views percolated downwards and are now almost common form. How was it done?

These earlier critical writings embody Mr Eliot's own search

[64]The fullest statement is in the essay on *Dante* (*S. E.* pp. 243-7).

[65]Preface to *The Sacred Wood* (second ed., 1928).

[66]For example, in *This Way to the Tomb* Ronald Duncan appears to have relied as much on the essay on Jonson as on *Murder in the Cathedral*.

as a poet for the material, no less than the principles, which would sustain him. His discovery of certain poets is also a discovery of his own powers: the relation of the essays on 'Andrew Marvell' and 'The Metaphysical Poets' to *The Waste Land*, of that on 'Lancelot Andrewes' to *Song for Simeon* and *Journey of the Magi*, of that on *Dante* to *Ash Wednesday* are so direct that the criticism is often the best commentary on the poetry.[67] When he stabilized his own style as a poet, some informing power departed from his critical writing. If for example the essay on 'In Memoriam' be compared with that on Massinger, or the introduction to the volume of Kipling's verse with the essay on Dryden, it will be seen that Mr Eliot has withdrawn from his subjects: he is no longer so closely engaged—this may allow a wider scale of social reference, but it weakens the characteristic virtue of his critical writing, which may be termed its involution. The portion of his criticism which records the growth of a poet's mind is also the portion which is germinal for his readers.[68]

Mr Eliot's method is determinate in his style; a neutral style, stripped of emotional phrase and metaphor though not without powerful resources of tone and inflexion, particularly the ironic. It is expository rather than forensic, and works much in terms of negatives, and of definition by exclusion:

> It is not so easy to see propriety in an image which divests a snake of *winter weeds*. . . .
> The difference is not a simple difference of degree between poets. . .
> We are baffled in the attempt to translate the quality indicated by the dim and antiquated term wit into the equally unsatisfactory nomenclature of our own times. . . .

A series of such qualifications and restrictions—

> *His Conversation so nicely*
> *Restricted to What Precisely*
> *And If and Perhaps and But*

—will start or terminate in a condensed statement ('what we

[67]Especially the passage on 'surprise' in 'Andrew Marvell', and the famous paragraph beginning 'The difference is not a simple difference of degree between poets' (*S. E.*, p. 273) in the essay on 'The Metaphysical Poets' may be related to *The Waste Land*: and the passage on the Divine Pageant (*S. E.*, pp. 248-50) in *Dante* related to *Ash Wednesday*.

[68]Cf. 'The Function of Criticism' (*S. E.*, p. 30) where only the reverse of this is conceded: Also, cf. 'The Perfect Critic' (*The Sacred Wood*, p. 15): 'The poetic critic is criticizing poetry in order to create poetry'.

have designated tentatively as wit, a tough reasonableness beneath the slight lyric grace'). The statement will gain meaning
and depth only in its context and in active conjunction with the
poetry of which it is predicated. Mr Eliot's style works by
reserves and implications—in his own phrase it has 'tentacular
roots'. This is its strength; and also of course its danger, for the
method allows play to assumptions and veils prejudices. But as
much could be said of other critical prose. The peculiar virtue
of Eliot's prose, its safeguard, and perhaps its intention is to involve the lively working co-operation of the reader. He does
not supply statements (however subtle) or communicate feelings
(however just and pertinent). He starts off a process. Either the
reader obtains very little from the criticism or he is himself
precipitated into activity. Mr Eliot employs criticism not to the
communication of truths but to the co-operative delineation of
the poetic experience.

The history of his views regarding the autonomy of the poetic
experience and the nature of the poetic experience have been
surveyed elsewhere. It is a corollary that in the earlier
period of his work Mr Eliot's criticism is criticism *tout pur*,
devoid of biographical, personal, sociological digressions:
devoid also of the residue of such imperfect creative impulses as
he discerns in some of the criticism of Coleridge and Symons:
devoid likewise of any debilitating rehash of what his author may
be supposed to 'mean'. [69]

> The labour of the intellect consisted largely in a purification, in
> keeping out a great deal . . . in refraining from reflection, in putting
> into the statement enough to make reflection unnecessary. . . . [70]

The precise quality of his author's achievement is elicited by
quotations in *alto-relievo*. The quotations are made to do the

---

[69] Criticism may reconstitute the work of art less because of an abortive
creative impulse in the critic than to accommodate the reader with a simplified substitute. Recently when reading aloud *Le Bateau Ivre* I was pressed to
say what it meant and replied with deliberate unhelpfulness that it meant
what it said, and, could other words suffice, it would not have been a successful poem at all. What was sought was a predigested version to avoid recourse
to the difficulties of the original. Even so general a remark as that it represented
the undifferentiated turmoil of feeling which is adolescence, the matrix of *all*
adult experience, would in the circumstances have been dangerous, an over-
stepping of 'the Function of Criticism'.

[70] 'The Possibility of Poetic Drama' (*The Sacred Wood*, p. 65).

critic's work, and the reader is made to work on them. They are more than 'happy quotations' in the usual sense: frequently they constitute Eliot's main statement. Against his reserved and restricted style they stand out, exactly chosen to make the point towards which he has been engaging the reader—but making it because the reader too is compelled to work over these particular lines, to respond actively to them, to relate to them all his own past experience of the writer under discussion.[71] Hence the strength with which Eliot's quotations stamp themselves on the mind of the reader and the frequency with which they pass into general circulation. Indeed the measure of activity and generative force in his quotations is the best index to the value of any particular essay.

In a celebrated passage the reader is invited to consider 'as a suggestive analogy, that action which takes place when a bit of finely filiated platinum is introduced into a chamber containing oxygen and sulphur dioxide'.[72] In turn I invite consideration of what happens when, under proper conditions, a single crystal is seeded into a non-crystalline mass of the same substance. All the patterned molecules, irregularly diffused, fall into the beautiful and intricate crystalline harmony of that single ordered unit: but the chemical constitution of either is in no way changed. Mr Eliot's criticism seeds the crystallization of the reader's existing knowledge and sensibility. In a sense nothing is added.[73] It is no substitute for the reading of literature: perhaps it is no more than the completion of the reader's own response: the final appreciation is a reciprocal affair.

> Choice being mutual act of all our souls
> Makes merit her election; and doth boil,
> As 'twere from forth us all, a man distill'd
> Out of our virtues.

[71] Cf. 'The Perfect Critic' (S. W., p. 11): '. . . In matters of great importance the critic must not coerce and he must not make judgements of worse and of better. He must simply elucidate: the reader will form the correct judgement for himself.' The fullest statement of this need for Negative Capability, and Mr Eliot's nearest approach to a manifesto is 'The Function of Criticism:' which is complemented rather than superseded by such a corrective as 'Religion and Literature.'

[72] 'Tradition and the Individual Talent' (S. E., p. 17).

[73] The pleasure is that which Aristotle called (in another connexion) Recognition: of saying 'Ah: that's it'. But the Recognition would not have come to the reader by himself.

Eliot's Critical Method

This happy conjunction is of course not inevitable or invariable, nor is it always invited. Mr Eliot has apologized for the 'pontifical solemnity' of some of his early writings.[74] Nervous stiffness and defensive irony were inevitable in an age when 'a complete severance between his poetry and *all* beliefs' could be imputed to him for righteousness.[75] The later criticism exhibits rather a haughty humility—'The poem *Gethsemane* (by Kipling) which I do not think I understand . . .'; the implication being, 'I expect you think it's simple, but that only shows how superficial your reading is'.[76]

His style is avowedly based upon the principle of Safety First: the essays in *Homage to John Dryden*

> in spite of, and partly because of, their defects preserve in cryptogram certain notions which, if expressed directly would be destined to immediate obloquy, followed by perpetual oblivion.[77]

Sometimes however Mr Eliot will state an honest disability so flatly that the too-cautious critic is taken unawares; as when he boggled at the imagery of

> *Keen as are the arrows*
> *Of that crystal sphere. . . .*[78]

or on the other hand in his respect for textual studies, he swallowed, hook, line and sinker, the work of the Disintegrators on *Hamlet*. His purely destructive work has sometimes been the result of some temperamental aversion: Milton has survived the attack of Mr Eliot and the Battle of the Critics which it provoked. (Yet how strange that a taste for Landor should accompany a distaste for Milton). In other cases it may have been deflected by the need for propaganda, for this motive appears more frequently in Eliot's iconoclastic writing. Hardy is rebuked for the delight in cruelty that is exhibited in *Barbara of the House of Grebe* whilst Kipling is exonerated by implication for '*The Mark of the Beast*—which those who do not believe in the existence of the Beast

[74]Preface to *The Sacred Wood* (2nd edition).

[75]I. A. Richards, *Science and Poetry* (1926), p. 64 (note). This provoked the controversy on Poetry and Belief and the statement was later modified by Dr Richards.

[76]Cf. also the note on Rymer to 'Hamlet and his Problems' (*S. E.*, p. 141), where however Mr Eliot is perhaps trailing his coat.

[77]Preface to the original edition (Hogarth Press, 1924).

[78]'A Note on Richard Crashaw' in *For Lancelot Andrewes* (1928), p. 123.

probably consider a beastly story'.[79] But in general, Eliot's destructive criticism has also anticipated the more general verdict, even as in the poems *Triumphal March* and *Difficulties of a Statesman* (1932) he anticipated the spirit of Nazi Germany and the spirit of Munich, with prophetic accuracy.

His equipment as a critic is congruent with his equipment as a poet: each reanimates the other.[80] In either case, their strength derives from the double endowment of a sense of language and a sense of structure. The period in which Mr Eliot began to write was one of almost unparalleled disintegration, and, though less afflicted, it was even more distressed than the world of to-day. The disillusion of the last post-war generation was such that the 'brilliant' writer—Lytton Strachey or Aldous Huxley—had only to exploit its fragmentary brightness and its protective cynicism to achieve success. In such a age, the artist finds a principle of order in the traditions of his art. Hence in his picture of the post-war chaos, *The Waste Land*—a picture of what it felt like to be alive in 1920 when most of your friends were dead—Eliot used the words of many dead poets as fragments to be shored against the ruins. They could provide the reckoning, the mental longitude and latitude, of which the age was incapable; he could apply them by selecting and placing, and thereby orientate himself. Each quotation implies its context and by condensing in this way, Mr Eliot was able to concentrate his vision of a whole society in disintegration. Since, however, it was a condition of this disintegration that there were no publically acceptable structural principles, no current literary conventions, he used the impressionist technique—later to be made familiar in the cinema—of a series of short sequences linked by a common theme only. This stage of his poetic writing is mirrored in the early criticism, where Mr Eliot is interested as a further attainment in large-scale structural pattern, as exhibited in Jonson, Dryden and Marlowe leading beyond the individual to the structure of Tradition; but as a nearer attainment in the local

[79] *After Strange Gods* (1934), p. 57, and Introduction to *A Choice of Kipling's Verse* (1941), p. 24. Personally I find both stories revolting, and belief in the Beast would not excuse Kipling's treatment, his relish of the torture. But Mr Eliot is concerned with the general standing of the two writers, trying to depress one and raise the other.

[80] Although, cf. *The Use of Poetry*, p. 30: 'The critical mind operating *in* poetry may always be in advance of the critical mind operating *upon* poetry.'

effects of language, the special qualities of vocabulary and rhythm in these writers, or in Massinger, Marvell, Swinburne or Shelley.[81] Here he is preoccupied with the way in which words work, as part of his own search for precision. This preoccupation appears even in his latest writing, e.g., in *Little Gidding*, V. To restore stability and fertility to words, out of the dustbowl of modern speech, has remained always Mr Eliot's *immediate* object as a writer, whatever the further object proposed. As it is by the study of language that he builds up the judgement of a simple poet, so it is by the essays on these individuals that he defines the Poetic Tradition he sought to re-establish. With no overt and formal unity, these scattered essays yet cohere into a single statement of principle, and require to be read *in extenso*.

The twin interests in structure and in language are best balanced in the essay on Dante which marks the end of Mr Eliot's exploratory phase in criticism. This essay appeared in 1929, the year before the publication of *Ash Wednesday*,[82] where he found both structure and vocabulary had come to him; soon after he was able to achieve so objective a form as the dramatic; and in his latest verse, critical reflection has been subsumed within the poetic form. The meditations on language in *Burnt Norton*, V, *East Coker* II and V, and *Little Gidding* II and V, do not suggest that any further critical *dicta* are likely to appear, and, after such poetry, there would be little point in Mr Eliot's expatiating on individuals, such as Dame Julian, whose influence is discernible in his verse. The process of involution is now complete, and 'there is namore to seye'. But by what he has done, both for the theory of literature—though he claims 'no gift whatever for abstruse thinking'[83]—and 'to bring the poet back to life—the great, the perennial task of criticism',[84] Eliot has set a standard

[81]Cf. 'The Possibility of a Poetic Drama' (*The Sacred Wood*, p. 63): 'To create or form is not merely to invent or shape, a rhyme or rhythm. It is also the realization of the whole appropriate content of this rhyme or rhythm. The sonnet of Shakespeare is not merely such and such a pattern but a precise way of thinking and feeling'.

[82]Single poems in this sequence had appeared earlier; 'Perch' io non Spero' (I) and 'Al Som de l'Escalina' (III) during 1928 and 1929 respectively.

[83]'Catholicism and International Order,' *Essays Ancient and Modern* (1936), p. 127. Mr Eliot is talking of economics, not of literature: and does not disclaim the ability to *generalize*.

[84]'Andrew Marvell' (*S. E.*, p. 278).

M. C. Bradbrook

and displayed a method to remain. In a definition of the twofold function of criticism he has himself remarked his double intention:

> There are these two theoretical limits of criticism: at one of which we attempt to answer the question 'What is poetry?' and at the other 'Is this a good poem?' No theoretical ingenuity will suffice to answer the second question because no theory can amount to much which is not founded upon a direct experience of good poetry: but on the other hand, our direct experience of poetry involves a good deal of generalizing activity.[85]

Although the progress of Mr Eliot's poetry may be traced in his critical preoccupations he has not confused his own practice and interests with those of the poets of whom he treats. That is to say, he has really approached the poets of the past as his masters, and with a desire to learn; and, apart from such exceptions as I have mentioned, his capacity to appreciate the virtues of writers who are personally uncongenial guarantees his integrity.[86] A 'concern' for letters (as the Friends would term it) distinguishes all his writing, and where his doctrinal interests intrude, they intrude quite frankly and may be therefore discounted by those who are in disagreement.

Critical playboys have been even more exasperated by Eliot the critic than by Eliot the poet, and have pilloried him as a species of literary Stafford Cripps, an advocate of Strength Through Misery. Although he has a pretty pen for such matters, Mr Eliot has not personally replied. With even sterner restraint he did not go beyond a general disclaimer of some of the views attributed to him by his admirers.

Mr Eliot's reputation as a critic in these twenty-five years has therefore not ripened like a cloudless dawn. The professors have not always been kind to him, and he has occasionally expressed some horror of universities. But perhaps among 'the gifts reserved for age' may be a juster sense in the public mind of the value of his critical achievement, for his method is one which requires to be assimilated, inducing not assent to a code, but the progress and growth of certain habits.

[85] *The Use of Poetry and the Use of Criticism* (1933), Introduction, p. 16.

[86] 'A very mature activity indeed' as he observes in 'A note on the development of Taste in poetry' (*The Use of Poetry*, p. 35) Cf. also 'Religion and Literature' (*Essays Ancient and Modern*, 1936), pp. 102-5, where he urges that *for the writer* his Christianity should inform the whole work but need not, perhaps had better not, be emergent: while *the critic* must not lose, though he must not commingle, his extra-literary criteria.

Notes on 'Gerontion'

GERONTION is concerned with the contrast between two attitudes; that which is expressed in the Duke's speech,[87] 'Be absolute for death', and that of the contemporary, who, involved in the general disintegration into 'Rocks, moss, stonecrop, iron, merds' is nevertheless compelled to protest, 'We have not reached conclusion'. The Duke's acceptance of death is, throughout the poem, implicitly opposed to the latter's rejection; the strength of the former's belief, enabling acceptance, is set against the paralysis of contemporary man who 'being old and rich, hath neither heat, affections, limb, nor beauty, to make his riches pleasant'.[88] And it is the whole nature of this contemporary barrenness which is examined in the course of an old man's reverie. As Dr Leavis has insisted, the poem 'has neither narrative nor logical continuity, and the only theatre in which the characters come together or could, is the mind of the old man'.[89] Gerontion, 'a representative human consciousness', is a character in a dramatic situation. He is not simply a projection of the poet's personality. Rather, he is the means whereby the poet effects 'an escape from personality' and the poem may, therefore, only be interpreted when its terms are related to the character, Gerontion, rather than to the poet himself.

The juxtaposition insisted upon by Elizabethan reminiscence throughout the poem is introduced at the outset with the contrast between the old man who has never participated in heroic action—action which is, symbolically, 'drenched' in

[87]The epigraph leads us to *Measure for Measure*, III, I, where the whole speech is clearly relevant to *Gerontion*.

[88]*Measure for Measure*, loc. cit.

[89]F. R. Leavis, *New Bearings in English Poetry*, pp. 83-84.

life-giving rain—and the boy whose innocent reading initiates Gerontion's reverie upon his own rainless condition, experience, and knowledge. It is a condition which is passive, unresistant to decay and dominated by a rootless, disinherited cosmopolitan culture.

> My house is a decayed house,
> And the jew squats on the window sill, the owner,

But this passivity has developed progressively from the point where action was possible;

> I was neither at the hot gates
> Nor fought in the warm rain
> Nor knee deep in the salt marsh, heaving a cutlass,
> Bitten by flies, fought.

The easy, supple movement of the fighting at the hot gates is slowed by the warm rain,[90] and then the action becomes much slower impeded by unproductive mud and salt, and preyed upon by the corrupting flies. The decayed house is the last figure in this progression away from uninhibited action. Its inhabitants and parts are equally decayed—Gerontion is infirm, the gutter is 'peevish', the woman sneezes, and the goat, archetype of potency is sick and coughing. Consummately the geography of the poem is established, a drab, impotent vista of inactivity;

> the owner,
> Spawned in some estaminet of Antwerp,
> Blistered in Brussels, patched and peeled in London.
> The goat coughs at night in the field overhead;
> Rocks, moss, stonecrop, iron, merds.
> The woman keeps the kitchen, makes tea,
> Sneezes at evening, poking the peevish gutter.
> I an old man,
> A dull head among windy spaces.

And Gerontion is placed clearly, a dominant and representative inhabitant of his country. There is, too, in this passage, a comment upon the loss of fertility through sexual failure. 'Spawned' in its associations with the breeding of the lower animals, suggests a repulsive promiscuous sexuality, a teeming like the Egyptian plague; while 'blistered', 'patched' and 'peeled' in conjunction with 'estaminet' imply the diseased debasement of brothels. But the reason for the infertility of

[90]The muscularity of these lines, too, suggests increasing effort.

Notes on 'Gerontion'

Gerontion is not to be found in this. The sexual corruption too, is the result of something deeper. The real reason is to be found in the contemporary repudiation of belief, and so far as this poem is concerned, of Christian belief. For although there may be a mechanical participation in the rites of Christianity or a passive intellectual acceptance of its dogmas, there is no 'passional' participation. Superstitious fear has supplanted innocent belief. The mob-demand for physical miracles cannot be satisfied with the subtle argument of Andrewes' 'verbum infans'. The complex wonder of the word of God invested in Christ, His own Word, a child incapable of speech, is the one miracle in which we cannot believe. And this refusal to believe in it, this blanketing of it by continual questioning, makes for a darkness which 'swaddles' the rejected truth;

> Signs are taken for wonders. 'We would see a sign!'
> The word within a word, unable to speak a word,
> Swaddled with darkness.

The mob incredulity and rejection of Christ is implicit in the Biblical reminiscence of the first line. And the babe invoked by 'swaddled' reinforces the association, making the nature of the repudiated 'word' specifically Christian, while the deliberate use of the image lends a concreteness to the preceding abstraction which should make the reference clear even to the reader who is not familiar with Lancelot Andrewes.

Technical acceptance of Christ is not so far from the flat rejection of the mob. The mechanical participation in the Sacrament;

> To be eaten, to be divided, to be drunk
> Among whispers;

is a 'sinister' and meaningless procedure, one of the 'signs' mistaken for the reality of redemption. The essential internal human demand for belief is not satisfied by this show, however, and there is a frustration in those who practise the deception, those who have paid-off 'religion', which occasions a nervousness for which they cannot account. The evasion indulged in

> by Mr. Silvero
> With caressing hands, at Limoges
> Who walked all night in the next room;

brings no quiescence. The connoisseur at an ancient shrine

131

makes some sort of gesture that fails to placate, and is consequently incapable of sleep. With similar discomfort, Hakagawa, the displaced oriental, makes ingratiating overtures to a foreign culture; de Tornquist[91] goes through her ritual with the candles in a spiritual 'dark room', and von Kulp is torn with indecision. All are picked out of the debris of the old man's reminiscences, and they belong to his own earlier condition of 'beauty lost in terror'. But at least these terrorized cosmopolitans are haunted by the beauty of a real belief. Gerontion has rationalized even his 'ghosts' away; having lost 'terror in inquisition' he discovers,

> I have no ghosts,
> An old man in a draughty house
> Under a windy knob.

These 'vacant shuttles' weaving the wind into the pattern of their society's destiny, are equally conspiratorial against the essential belief, for either through enquiry or the acceptance of substitutes they deny 'Christ the tiger'. They represent admirably the end-products of the historical 'year'[92] of the Christian era, the twenty post-Christian centuries represented as a sort of year with a seasonal rise and fall;

> In the juvescence of the year
> Came Christ the tiger

> In depraved May, dogwood and chestnut, flowering judas,

The ethos has enormous potency and vitality at the time of the first utterance of the Word. But after the Easter-time crucifixion of the tiger, the late spring of the Christian 'year' becomes 'depraved',[93] weeds flourish,[94] the phallic spikes of chestnut are rampant—a regression in pagan terms—and the betrayer of Christ flourishes again in the 'flowering' of his tree. With the consequent Christianity of whispers, the reduction of the tiger is apparently completed. But there is inevitably a new 'year'. Originally the 'tiger' came to us gently, in our interest. After

[91]The suggestiveness of these names has been commented upon before and the fact points the highly conscious nature of the poem.

[92]The image of the year is suggested also by the 'dry month'

[93]Dr. Leavis has noted the close similarity this image bears in realization with 'Lilies that fester' of Shakespeare's sonnet.

[94]The highly conscious selection of the weed 'dogweed', anticipate Mr. Eliot's later use of the Dog archetype in *The Waste Land* and *Marina*. The effect here is the clear definition of the 'weeds'.

'our impudent crimes' and the 'unnatural vices' for which we are responsible, its attitude towards us has changed. In the 'Second Coming', in the 'new year', the tiger 'springs' and it is 'us he devours', completing inevitably and mercilessly the historic cycle.

> *The tiger springs in the new year.   Us he devours.*

All are to be destroyed. Gerontion's tortured acceptance, and Mr Silvero's passive ritual have about the same value. They are part of the same pathology of disbelief.

The devouring is already partially accomplished by the fear which has supplanted the beauty of passional belief;

> *I that was near your heart was removed therefrom*
> *To lose beauty in terror, terror in inquisition.*

Fear is common both to the cosmopolitans who clearly manifest it and to Gerontion, who claims that he has 'lost' it. For if Gerontion's 'inquisition' has revealed anything, if his old man's exploration has discovered some end at all, it is surely the need to be 'absolute for death', to 'encounter darkness as a bride' as Claudio is urged to encounter it. However, all Gerontion's discoveries proceed towards a point where the necessity for absolute acceptance is intellectually conceded, and at that point veer away into rationalization, for the fear is still there. The demand for death should logically follow his several statements of complete infertility, but an old man's persistent grip upon life asserts itself in spite of this deep need. We have instead, the rhetorical assertion

> *Think at last*
> *We have not reached conclusion, when I*
> *Stiffen in a rented house. Think at last*
> *I have not made this show purposelessly*
> *And it is not by any concitation*
> *Of the backward devils.*

When the immediately preceding realization has been,

> *Us he devours.*

and the whole examination has certainly demonstrated the essential 'purposelessness' of the 'show'. Further those 'backward devils' who have consistently rejected Christ *are* conspiratorial and consequently responsible for the inadequate show,

Wolf Mankowitz

an inadequacy fully acknowledged by Gerontion's later comment,

Tenants of the house.[95]
Thoughts of a dry brain in a dry season.

His attempt, then, to depersonalize himself has been only partly successful. He can probably with considerable truth—being after all, an old man—say,

I have lost my sight, smell, hearing, taste and touch;
How should I use them for your closer contact?

but the comment is more an irony of the poet than a conclusion of the poem; it is a comment in character. Gerontion's humanity remains for the one reason that he is unable to accept death 'which makes these odds all even'; it is the characteristic which makes him representative'.

The whole of Gerontion's complex inquisition really would seem to constitute an apology for his failure to passionally believe, or having intellectually conceded the required belief, his constitutional inability to accept its corollary in faith. This apology is directed in the way that a believer's prayer would be directed towards the accepted godhead. But unlike the believer's credo, unconditional and accepting, Gerontion's address is an intellectual one intended to persuade an intellectually conceived god. And the central portion of his reverie is consistent rhetorical persuasion. It is the paradox of Gerontion's position which paralyses, for while his deliberations can lead him to reject the intellectual powers which direct them, he is still, in the very act of rejection, a creature of those powers. He is able only to know, and only in knowing state;

After such knowledge, what forgiveness?

but immediately he must find reasons qualifying himself for that very forgiveness. In the protracted apostrophe to the godhead he implies by argument his qualification, but it is the manner of address which he adopts—'Think now', and 'I would meet you upon this honestly'—which would seem to

[95]It is difficult to know what Dr. Richards intends by his comment, 'The next two lines . . . are almost an excuse'. It would seem rather that they have a very real place in a deliberate organization which may be 'magic' but certainly cannot be, as he suggests, immediately 'responded to'. *Principles of Literary Criticism*, p. 293.

Notes on 'Gerontion'

indicate his real attitude;

> *Think now*
> *History has many cunning passages, contrived corridors*
> *And issues, deceives with whispering ambitions,*
> *Guides us by vanities.*

Though the predetermined end of the effort of human beings within the historical progression is suggested, Gerontion still knows that there can be no excuse; the tiger cannot be appeased for his devouring is right and inevitable. But the argument is compelling, and must be followed through. As well as an apology it is an explanation of why Gerontion must be devoured. 'History' becomes for him a temptress enticing him on into the jaws of the tiger;

> *She gives when our attention is distracted*
> *And what she gives, gives with such supple confusions*
> *That the giving famishes the craving.*

However, the intellectual faculty quickly picks up the qualities of History the temptress, and drives them beyond a personal application in emotional terms. The tone of,

> *Gives too late*
> *What's not believed in, or if still believed*
> *In memory only, reconsidered passion.*

has become cooler. Gerontion has accepted the need for belief in the latter years of his life, but with his contemporaries, all equi-distant from 'the juvescence of the year' can possess only a 'receipt for deceit' in his inwardly dead acceptance of the belief. The rejection of Christ is recollected again, and the origin of the sense of guilt accounted for as a revenge for refusing Christianity.

> *Gives too soon*
> *Into weak hands, what's thought can be dispensed with*
> *Till the refusal propagates a fear.*

The final term of the Gerontion paralysis is also the first term of all sin, and it is 'such knowledge' which insists upon the inevitable ill-effects of any action—even the naïve heroism of the Thermopylæ battle 'saving civilization'—

> *Think*
> *Neither fear nor courage saves us. Unnatural vices*
> *Are fathered by our heroism. Virtues*

135

Wolf Mankowitz

Are forced upon us by our impudent crimes.
These tears are shaken from the wrath-bearing tree.

The accretion of images of sexual violence culminating in the 'naked vision' of the Eden-tree[96] supports the previous undertone of the poem's comment upon the unhealthily fertile 'richness' of corruption. 'Unnatural' is picked up by 'fathered', and the implied monsters to echo the earlier associations of 'spawned'. At the same time 'forced' and 'impudent crimes' comment upon the nature of the 'fathering', and the resultant 'tears' 'remind thee of thy mother's grief' beneath 'the wrath-bearing tree'. The remarkable use of the evocative powers of the implicit imagery in these lines, the extension of the poem insisted upon by the miraculous control of association and suggestion, are qualities of achievement rarely encountered anywhere in literature. The qualities of Gerontion's situation, with its contradictions and complexities, are organized with astonishing certainty, a certainty which often anticipates the maturity of Mr Eliot's latest work.

The irony of *Gerontion* is never obtrusive. The distance from experience which the poet's use of dramatic soliloquy enables him to achieve prevents his technique from ever becoming obvious. But clearly the protagonist is conceived ironically and seen from the poet's distance, the irony is that of Gerontion's knowledge of the need for action, without any of the propensities for it. The rhetoric noted above, 'the general mess of imprecision', contributes to an effect which is not, in spite of the specific nature of the summing-up, 'Thoughts of a dry brain', immediate in action. It is an effect which progressively asserts itself as the poem is assimilated. There is never any slickly direct advertisement of the poet's personal position or attitude, and consequently a higher degree of consciousness is demanded of the reader if he is to recognize the presence of the central irony at all. In the concluding part of the poem the use of 'small' and 'chilled' assert the point, while the image 'protract the profit' puts the whole of Gerontion's 'deliberations upon a figurative commercial basis—an old man's effort to get the

[96]The similarity this image bears to Blake's 'naked visions' of the Tree's significance is certainly conscious—the 'Poison Tree' is wrath which 'did grow', 'watered with tears'.

most out of his superannuated 'delirium';

> These with a thousand small deliberations
> Protract the profit of their chilled delirium,
> Excite the membrane, when the sense has cooled,
> With pungent sauces, multiply variety
> In a wilderness of mirrors.

The sharp, artificially-induced intellectual excitement also palls, and the dream implications of 'delirium' are extended in the image 'wilderness of mirrors', a confusion which grows towards the end of the poem. Into Gerontion's consciousness floats the literary reminiscence of

> What will the spider do,
> Suspend its operations, will the weevil
> Delay?

It is, again, a disguised expression of the death Gerontion refuses to mention directly. The spatial sensation of

> De Bailhache, Fresca, Mrs. Cammel, whirled[97]
> Beyond the circuit of the shuddering Bear
> In fractured atoms.

is also of the dream world, and like the preceding lines bears a rationalized expression of death, the euphemistic 'fractured atoms'. Annihilation is softened by the suggestion of other existence in far off space beyond the constellations. The dream belongs to the literal 'after-dinner sleep' into which Gerontion seems to be slipping. Into the trailing phantasy before he becomes completely 'at-one' with his 'sleepy corner', Gerontion's memories slip;

> Gull against the wind, in the windy straits
> Of Belle Isle, or running on the Horn,
> White feathers in the snow, the Gulf claims,

They are loosely associated, the straits suggesting Belle Isle, and the isle, the Horn—'the only theatre in which they come together, or could, is the mind of the old man'. But the baffled helpless gull, and the suggestion of unresistance in 'running', are clearly symbolic of the situation defined by the

---

[97]The effect here is perhaps comparable with that of
> And blown with restless violence round about
> The pendent world;
>> *Measure for Measure*, III, I.

Wolf Mankowitz

whole poem; the 'white feathers' of the bird buried in the snow they suggest express, as directly as is possible for Gerontion, his deep desire for oblivion and death. The unrelated 'the Gulf claims' is reminiscent of Mr Eliot's later technique, as in the lines;

> For Thine is
> Life is
> For Thine is the

and here successfully recaptures the logical disjointedness, but symbolic relevance, of the drift in a pre-sleep phantasy. All the images in the passage belong to the geography of Gerontion's mind, and—it can hardly be insisted too often—only have meaning when considered in that context. 'The Gulf claims' is then as final a summing up of the situation as are the concluding two lines of the poem. The consignment to the Gulf of all parties to the 'chilled delirium' plays against the more conscious rationalism of 'Tenants of the house', and this controlled juxtaposition is another example of the remarkably high degree of consciousness behind the poem, which concludes with a final reference to the awaited rain mentioned in the first lines of the poem. And the 'Trades' are now seen to be not only the actual winds which have driven the old man into a decayed house for protection, but also the seasonally renewed vigour of 'Christ the tiger', and Gerontion's own self-destructive 'fertility' of enquiry.

Such an analysis as this paper attempts may well be 'impudent' and certainly cannot be exhaustive. It can, however, point the controlled nature of a poem which has been generally neglected, and which (though this is the subject of another paper, perhaps) shows signs of the later development of the Quartets in ways which are startling for the pre-Waste Land period of Mr Eliot's achievement. Further, it is difficult to know how so complex a work as *Gerontion* can be approached other than through the most detailed written examination. It is a consummate example of that writing with 'the intellect at the tips of the senses' of which Mr Eliot speaks in the essay on Massinger, and such writing will always demand the enthusiasm of concentrated reading, rather than that of adjectival recommendation.

A CHECK LIST OF T. S. ELIOT'S PUBLISHED WRITINGS

This list deals with books written entirely by T. S. Eliot or containing contributions by him. A necessarily incomplete list of Mr Eliot's contributions to periodicals is added. References, except where otherwise stated, are to first editions: but to save space the first English and American editions of a book, with subsequent editions (when these are of special interest), are mentioned in the same entry. Contributions to periodicals are usually not listed when they are available in books, and books with other contributions besides Mr Eliot's are not listed, when Mr Eliot's contribution is available in a book written entirely by him. Earlier texts of Mr Eliot's collected poems (but not of his collected prose) are recorded in the appropriate entry. Unsigned and pseudonymous writings are listed only when they have been ascribed elsewhere to Mr Eliot.

I am greatly indebted to Donald C. Gallup's *A Catalogue of English and American First Editions of Writings by T. S. Eliot* (New Haven, 1937). Readers requiring more detailed description than is possible in this check list should consult Mr Gallup's bibliography.

I

COLLECTED POEMS

1   *Prufrock and other Observations.* The Egoist Ltd., London, 1917.
Reprints 'The Love Song of Alfred J. Prufrock' from *Poetry* [Chicago], June 1915, 'Preludes' and 'Rhapsody of a Windy Night' from *Blast*, July 1915, 'Portrait of a Lady' from *Others*, September 1915, 'Cousin Nancy' from *Poetry* [Chicago], October 1915, 'Aunt Helen' and 'Hysteria' from Ezra Pound's *Catholic Anthology* (London, November 1915), and 'Morning at the Window', 'Conversation Galante', 'Mr Apollinax' and 'La Figlia che Piange' from *Poetry* [Chicago], September 1916.

T. S. Eliot

2   *Poems*. The Hogarth Press, Richmond, 1919.

      Reprints 'Le Spectateur' (originally 'Le Directeur'), 'Lune de Miel', 'Mélange Adultère de Tout' and 'The Hippopotamus' from *The Little Review*, July 1917, and 'Sweeney among the Nightingales', 'Mr Eliot's Sunday Morning Service', and 'Whispers of Immortality', from *The Little Review*, September 1918.

3   *Ara Vus* [sic] *Prec*. The Ovid Press, London, 1920.

      Edition limited to 264 copies, of which 10 were for review, 4 specially bound and not for sale, 30 numbered and signed by the author, and 220 numbered but unsigned.

      Reprints 1 and 2, deleting 'Hysteria'. Also reprints 'Ode' from *The Harvard Advocate*, 24 June 1910, 'The Boston Evening Transcript' from *Poetry* [Chicago], October 1915 and Ezra Pound's *Catholic Anthology* (1915), 'Dans le Restaurant' from *The Little Review*, September 1918, 'A Cooking Egg' from *Coterie*, May-Day 1919, and 'Burbank with a Baedeker: Bleistein with a Cigar' and 'Sweeney Erect' from *Art and Letters*, Summer 1919. Also adds 'Gerontion'.

      The error 'Vus' for 'Vos' appears on the title-page but is corrected on the label.

4   *Poems*. Alfred A. Knopf, New York, 1920.

      Reprints 3, substituting 'Hysteria' for 'Ode'.

5   *The Waste Land*. Boni and Liveright, New York, 1922 (edition limited to 1,000 copies). The Hogarth Press, Richmond, 1923.

      The poem first appeared in *The Criterion*, October 1922 and in *The Dial*, November 1922. It was printed unknown to the author in 'Prize Poems 1913-29. Edited by Charles A. Wagner' (Charles Boni Paper Books, New York, 1930), the U.S.A. copyright having been sold by Liveright to Boni. The author was only informed of the transaction later.

6   *Poems 1909-25*. Faber and Gwyer, London, 1925. Harcourt Brace, New York, 1932.

      Faber and Gwyer also published, in 1926, a limited edition of 85 signed copies.

      Reprints 4 and 5 adding 'The Hollow Men'. Earlier drafts of this poem can be found in *The Chapbook*, 1924, *Commerce*, Winter 1924, *The Criterion*, January 1925, and *The Dial*, March 1925.

7   *Journey of the Magi*. Faber and Gwyer, London, 1927. Ariel Poems No. 8. Also a limited edition of 350 copies. William Edwin Rudge, New York, 1927. Limited edition of 27 copies.

Check List

8   *A Song for Simeon*. Faber and Gwyer, London, 1928. Ariel Poems No. 16. Also a limited edition of 500 signed copies.

9   *Animula*. Faber and Faber, London, 1928. Ariel Poems No. 23. Also a limited edition of 400 signed copies.

10   *Ash-Wednesday*. Faber and Faber, London, and The Fountain Press, New York, 1930. Limited to 600 signed copies, 200 for sale in Great Britain and 400 for sale in the U.S.A. Trade edition by Faber and Faber, 1930. First American trade edition by G. P. Putnam's Sons and The Knickerbocker Press, New York, 1930.
     Reprints as Part I 'Perch' io non Spero' from *Commerce*, Spring 1928, as Part II 'Salutation' from *The Saturday Review of Literature*, 10 December 1927 and *The Criterion*, January 1928, and as Part III, 'Al Som de l'Escalina' from *Commerce*, Autumn 1929. There are several changes in the text.

11   *Marina*. Faber and Faber, London, 1930. Ariel Poems No. 28. Also a limited edition of 400 signed copies.

12   *Triumphal March*. Faber and Faber, London, 1931. Ariel Poems No. 35. Also a limited edition of 400 signed copies.

13   *Sweeney Agonistes. Fragments of an Aristophanic Melodrama*. Faber and Faber, London, 1932.
     Reprints 'Fragments of a Prologue' from *The Criterion*, October 1926 and 'Fragments of an Agon' from *The Criterion*, January 1927.

14   *Words for Music*. Printed by Frederic Prokosch at the Bryn Mawr Press, Bryn Mawr, Pennsylvania, February 1934. Edition limited to 22 copies. Also available in *The Best Poems of* 1934 (Jonathan Cape, London and Toronto. Harcourt Brace, New York) and in *The Virginia Quarterly Review*, April 1934.

15   *The Rock. A Pageant Play*. Faber and Faber, London, 1934. Harcourt Brace, New York, 1934.

16   *Murder in the Cathedral*. Friends of Canterbury Cathedral edition, H. J. Goulden Limited, Canterbury, 1935.
     This 'slightly abbreviated acting edition for the Festival of the Friends of Canterbury Cathedral' precedes the Faber edition and the first American edition by Harcourt Brace.

17   *Two Poems*. Printed by Frederic Prokosch at the Cambridge University Press, October 1935. Edition limited to 22 copies.
     The two poems are 'Cape Ann' and 'Usk'.

18   *Collected Poems* 1909-35. Faber and Faber, London, 1935. Harcourt Brace, New York, 1935.

Reprints 6, 7, 8, 9, 10, 11, 12, 13, 14, the choruses from 15, and 17. Adds 'Eyes that last I saw in Tears' from *The Criterion*, January 1925, 'Difficulties of a Statesman' from *The Hound and Horn*, Autumn 1932, and *Commerce*, Winter 1932, 'Five finger Exercises' from *The Criterion* January 1933 and 'Rannoch by Glencoe' from *The New English Weekly*, 17 October 1935 and *New Democracy*, 15 December 1935. Also includes 'Lines for an Old Man' and 'Burnt Norton'.

19 *The Family Reunion*. Faber and Faber, London, 1939. Harcourt Brace, New York, 1939.

20 *Old Possum's Book of Practical Cats*. Faber and Faber, London, 1939. Harcourt Brace, New York, 1939. Edition illustrated by Nicholas Bentley, Faber and Faber, 1939.

21 *East Coker*. Faber and Faber, London, 1940.
    Reprinted from *The New English Weekly*, 21 March 1940.

22 *Burnt Norton*. Faber and Faber, London, 1941.
    Reprinted from 18.

23 *The Dry Salvages*. Faber and Faber, London, 1941.
    Reprinted from *The New English Weekly*, 27 February 1941.

24 *Little Gidding*. Faber and Faber, London, 1942.
    Reprinted from *The New English Weekly*, 15 October 1942.

25 *Four Quartets*. Harcourt Brace, New York, 1943. Faber and Faber, London, 1944.
    Reprints 21, 22, 23 and 24 with slight alterations. The first issue of the first edition [New York, 1943] (distinguishable from subsequent issues by the words 'first edition' on the verso of the title-page) is rare. It was immediately withdrawn after publication and replaced by a typographically superior second issue.

II

UNCOLLECTED POEMS

(Nos. 26-34 have been reprinted in December 1938 issue of *The Harvard Advocate*)

26 'Song.' *The Harvard Advocate*, 24 May 1907.

27 'Song.' *The Harvard Advocate*, 3 June 1907.

28 'Before Morning.' *The Harvard Advocate*, 13 November 1908.

29 'Circe's Palace.' *The Harvard Advocate*, 25 November 1908.

30 'Song.' *The Harvard Advocate*, 26 January 1909.

Check List

31 'On a Portrait.' *The Harvard Advocate*, 26 January 1909.

32 'Nocturne.' *The Harvard Advocate*, 12 November 1909.

33 'Humoresque.' *The Harvard Advocate*, 12 January 1910.

34 'Spleen.' *The Harvard Advocate*, 26 January 1910.

35 'To the Indians who Died in Africa.' *Queen Mary's Book for India*, Harrap, London, 1943, p.61.

36 'A Note on Poetry in Wartime.' *London Calling*, edited by Storm Jameson. Harper, New York, 1942.

III

COLLECTED PROSE

37 *Ezra Pound. His Metric and Poetry.* Alfred A. Knopf, New York, 1917. Published anonymously.

38 *The Sacred Wood. Essays on Poetry and Criticism.* Methuen, London, 1920. Alfred A. Knopf, New York, 1921. Second edition, with new preface, Methuen, 1928.

39 *Homage to John Dryden. Three Essays on the Poetry of the Seventeenth Century.* The Hogarth Press, London, 1924.

40 *Shakespeare and the Stoicism of Seneca. An Address read before the Shakespeare Association.* Oxford University Press, London, 1927.

41 *For Lancelot Andrewes. Essays on Style and Order.* Faber and Gwyer, London, 1928. Doubleday Doran, New York, 1929.

42 *Dante.* Faber and Faber, London, 1929. Also a limited edition of 125 signed copies.

43 *Thoughts after Lambeth.* Faber and Faber, London, 1931.

44 *Charles Whibley. A Memoir.* The English Association. Pamphlet No. 80. Oxford University Press, London, 1931.

45 *Selected Essays.* Faber and Faber, London, 1932. Also a limited edition of 115 signed copies. Harcourt Brace, New York, 1932. Reprints with additions part of 38, 39, 40, part of 41, 42, 43 and 44. A second edition by Faber in 1934 adds an essay on Marston.

46 *John Dryden. The Poet. The Dramatist. The Critic.* Terence and Elsa Holliday, New York, 1932. Also a limited edition of 110 signed copies.

47 *The Use of Poetry and the Use of Criticism.* Faber and Faber, London, 1933. Harvard University Press, Cambridge, Mass., 1933.

48 *After Strange Gods. A Primer of Modern Heresy*. Faber and Faber, London, 1934. Harcourt Brace, New York, 1934.

49 *Elizabethan Essays*. Faber and Faber, London, 1934.
> Reprints Part III of 45. Adds an essay on Marston which is also added in the 1934, London edition of 45.

50 *Essays Ancient and Modern*. Faber and Faber, London, 1936. Harcourt Brace, New York, 1936.
> Reprints four essays from 41. Adds six essays hitherto uncollected.

51 *The Idea of a Christian Society*. Faber and Faber, London, 1939. Harcourt Brace, New York, 1940.

52 *Points of View* (edited by John Hayward). Faber and Faber, London, 1941.
> A selection from Eliot's criticism.

53 *The Music of Poetry*. Jackson, Son and Son, Glasgow, 1942.
> The W. P. Ker Memorial Lecture for 1942. Also in *Partisan Review*, November-December, 1942.

54 *The Classics and the Man of Letters*. Oxford University Press, London, 1942.
> The Presidential Address to the Classical Association, 15 April 1942.

55 *Reunion by Destruction. Reflections on a Scheme for Church Union in South India*. Pamphlet No. 7 of the Council for the Defence of Church Principles, Dacre House, Westminster, 1944.

56 *What is a Classic?* Faber and Faber, London, 1945.
> The Presidential Address to the Virgil Society, October 1944.

IV

UNCOLLECTED PROSE. PREFACES, INTRODUCTIONS AND FOREWORDS
(Material available in Nos. 37-56 is not listed)

57 *Le Serpent;* by Paul Valery. With a translation into English by Mark Wardle. Cobden-Sanderson, London, 1924. Edition limited to 525 copies.
> 'A Brief Introduction to the Method of Paul Valery', by T. S. Eliot, pp. 7-15.

58 *Savanarola. A Dramatic Poem;* by Charlotte Eliot. Cobden-Sanderson, London, 1926.
> 'Introduction', by T. S. Eliot, pp. VII-XII.

Check List

- 59 *This American World;* by Edgar Ansell Mowrer. Faber and Gwyer, London, 1928.
  'Preface', by T. S. Eliot, pp. ix-xv.

- 60 *Fishermen of the Banks;* by J. B. Conolly. Faber and Gwyer, London, 1928.
  The preface is by T. S. Eliot.

- 61 *Ezra Pound. Selected Poems;* edited by T. S. Eliot. Faber and Gwyer, London, 1928. Ordinary edition and limited edition of 100 signed copies.
  'Introduction', by T. S. Eliot, pp. vii-xxv.

- 62 *The Wheel of Fire. Essays in Interpretation of Shakespeare's Sombre Tragedies;* by G. Wilson Knight. Oxford University Press, London, 1930.
  'Introduction', by T. S. Eliot, pp. xi-xix.

- 63 *'London': A Poem and 'The Vanity of Human Wishes';* by Samuel Johnson. Etchells and Macdonald, London, 1930. Limited to 150 signed and 300 unsigned copies.
  'Introductory Essay', by T. S. Eliot, pp. 9-17.

- 64 *Anabasis;* a poem by St J. Perse. With a translation into English by T. S. Eliot. Faber and Faber, London, 1930. Ordinary edition and edition limited to 350 signed copies. The text of the first American edition (Harcourt Brace, 1938) was revised by the author and John Hayward.
  'Preface', by T. S. Eliot, pp. 7-11 of English edition.

- 65 *Transit of Venus;* Poems by Harry Crosby. The Black Sun Press, Paris, 1931. Limited to 20 lettered and 50 numbered copies together with sheets for 500 copies.
  'Preface', by T. S. Eliot, pp. i-ix.

- 66 *Bubu of Montparnasse;* by Charles Louis Phillippe. Translated by Lawrence Vail. Crosby Continental Editions, Paris, 1932.
  'Preface', by T. S. Eliot, pp. vii-xiv.

- 67 *The Collected Poems of Harold Monro;* edited by Alida Monro. Cobden-Sanderson, London, 1933.
  'Critical Note', by T. S. Eliot, pp. xiii-xvi.

- 68 *Selected Poems by Marianne Moore.* The Macmillan Company, New York, 1935. Faber and Faber, London, 1935.
  'Introduction', by T. S. Eliot, pp. vii-xiv of American and pp. 5-12 of English edition.

- 69 *Nightwood;* by Djuna Barnes. [Faber and Faber, London, 1936.] Harcourt Brace, New York, 1937.
  The American edition has a preface by T. S. Eliot.

70 *The Testament of Immortality;* An Anthology. Faber and Faber, London, 1940.
      'Foreword', by T. S. Eliot.

71 *A Little Book of Modern Verse;* edited by Anne Ridler. Faber and Faber, London, 1941.
      'Preface', by T. S. Eliot, pp. 5-9.

72 *A Choice of Kipling's Verse;* selected by T. S. Eliot. Faber and Faber, London, 1942.
      'Rudyard Kipling', by T. S. Eliot, pp. 5-36.

73 *Introducing James Joyce;* a selection of his prose by T. S. Eliot. Faber and Faber, London, 1942.
      'Introductory Note', by T. S. Eliot, pp. 5-7.

74 *Shakespeare and the Popular Dramatic Tradition;* by S. L. Bethell. Staples and Staples, London, 1944.
      'Introduction', by T. S. Eliot, pp. [7-9].

75 *Inoubliable France;* by Alice Jahier. Translated by J. G. Weightman. The Sylvan Press, London, 1944.
      'To the Reader', by T. S. Eliot, p. [I].

V

UNCOLLECTED PROSE. CONTRIBUTIONS TO BOOKS

(Material available in Nos. 37-75 is not listed)

76 'Experiment in Criticism.' *Tradition and Experiment in Present Day Literature.* Oxford University Press, London, 1929.

77 'Religion Without Humanism.' *Humanism and America*, edited by Norman Foerster. Farrar and Rinehart, New York, 1930.

78 'Donne in our Time.' *A Garland for John Donne*, edited by Theodore Spencer. Harvard University Press, Cambridge, Mass., 1931.

79 'Shakespearean Criticism: I. From Dryden to Coleridge.' *A Companion to Shakespeare Studies*, edited by Harley Granville-Barker and G. B. Harrison. Cambridge University Press, 1934.

80 'A Note on the Verse of John Milton'. *Essays and Studies of the English Association*, Vol. XXI. Collected by Herbert Read. The Clarendon Press, Oxford, 1936.

81 *Revelation*, edited by John Baillie and Hugh Martin. Faber and Faber, London, 1937.
      Contains untitled essay on revelation by T. S. Eliot.

82 'Byron.' *From Anne to Victoria*, edited by Bonamy Dobrée. Cassell, London, 1937.

83 'A Note on Two Odes of Cowley.' *Seventeenth Century Studies Presented to Sir Herbert Grierson*. Oxford University Press, London, 1938.

84 *Britain at War*, edited by Monroe Wheeler. Museum of Modern Art, New York, 1941.
Text by T. S. Eliot and others.

85 'The Christian Conception of Education.' *The Proceedings of the Archbishop of York's Conference, Malvern*, 1941. Longmans, London, 1941.

86 'The Nature of Cultural Relations.' *Friendship, Progress, Civilization*. Three War-time Speeches to the Anglo-Swedish Society, 1943.

87 'Cultural Forces in the Human Order.' *Prospect for Christendom*, edited by M. B. Reckitt. Faber and Faber, London, 1945.

88 *The Crack-Up*. A selection from the letters, notebooks and uncollected papers of F. Scott Fitzgerald, edited by Edmund Wilson. New Directions, New York, 1945.
Includes a letter from T. S. Eliot.

VI

UNCOLLECTED PROSE. CONTRIBUTIONS TO PERIODICALS

(Material available in Nos. 37-88 is not listed. Correspondence is only listed selectively and broadcasts are not listed at all)

1909

[A review of] 'The Wine of the Puritans', by Van Wyck Brooks, *The Harvard Advocate*, 7 May 1909.
The Point of View. *The Harvard Advocate*, 20 May 1909.
Gentleman and Seaman. *The Harvard Advocate*, 25 May 1909.

1916

[A review of] 'Theism and Humanism', by A. J. Balfour. *Int. Jour. of Ethics*, January 1916.
[A review of] 'The philosophy of Nietzsche', by A. Wolf. *Int. Jour. of Ethics*, April 1916.
[A review of] 'Group Theories of Religion and the Individual', by C. J. Webb. *Int. Jour. of Ethics*, October 1916.
[A review of] 'Conscience and Christ', by H. Rashdall. *Int. Jour. of Ethics*, October 1916.

T. S. Eliot

The Development of Leibniz's Monadism. *Monist*, October 1916.
Leibniz's Monads and Bradley's Finite Centres. *Monist*, October 1916.
Classics in English. *Poetry* [Chicago], November 1916.

1917

[A review of] 'Elements of Folk Psychology', by W. Wundt. Translated by E. L. Schaub. *Int. Jour. of Ethics*, January 1917.
Reflections on Vers Libre. *New Statesman*, 3 March 1917.
The Borderline of Prose. *New Statesman*, 19 May 1917.
The Letters of J. B. Yeats. *Egoist*, July 1917.
The Noh and the Image. *Egoist*, August 1917.
Reflections on Contemporary Poetry, I-III. *Egoist*, September, October, November 1917.
Turgenev. *Egoist*, December 1917.

1918

Recent British Periodical Literature in Ethics. *Int. Jour. of Ethics*, January 1917.
In Memory of Henry James. *The Egoist*, January 1918 and *The Little Review*, August 1918.
Literature and the American Courts. *Egoist*, March 1918.
Verse Pleasant and Unpleasant. *Egoist*, March 1918.
Disjecta Membra. *Egoist*, April 1918.
Professional or. . . . *Egoist*, April 1918. (Signed Apteryx.)
Contemporanea. *Egoist*, June-July 1918.
Observations. *Egoist*, May 1918. (Signed Apteryx.)
The Hawthorne Aspect. *Little Review*, August 1918.
Short Notices. *Egoist*, August 1918.
'Tarr.' *Egoist*, September 1918.
A Note on Ezra Pound. *Today*, September 1918.
Studies in Contemporary Criticism, I-II. *Egoist*, November-December 1918.

1919

Marivaux. *Art and Letters*, Spring 1919.
American Literature. *Athenaeum*, 25 April 1919.
A Romantic Patrician. *Athenaeum*, 2 May 1919.
Kipling Redivivus. *Athenaeum*, 9 May 1919.
A Sceptical Patrician. *Athenaeum*, 23 May 1919.
Kipling Redivivus. [A letter] To the Editor. *Athenaeum*, 16 May 1919.
Beyle and Balzac. *Athenaeum*, 30 May 1919.
Eeldrop and Appleplex, I-II. *Little Review*, May, September, 1919.
Part I pirated in *Two Worlds Monthly*, September 1926.
Criticism in England. *Athenaeum*, 13 June 1919.

Check List

The Education of Taste. *Athenaeum*, 27 June 1919.

A Foreign Mind. *Athenaeum*, 4 July 1919.

Reflections on Contemporary Poetry, IV. *Egoist*, July 1919.

The Romantic Generation if it Existed. *Athenaeum*, 18 July 1919.

Whether Rostand had something about Him. *Athenaeum*, 25 July 1919.

Was there a Scottish Literature? *Athenaeum*, 1 August 1919.

Swinburne and the Elizabethans. *Athenaeum*, 19 September 1919.

Humanist Artist and Scientist. *Athenaeum*, 10 October 1919.

War Paint and Feathers. *Athenaeum*, 17 October 1919.

Our Inaccessible Heritage. [A letter] To the Editor. *Athenaeum*, 24 October 1919.

The Method of Mr Pound. *Athenaeum*, 24 October 1919.

The Comedy of Humours. *Athenaeum*, 14 November 1919.

The Preacher as Artist. *Athenaeum*, 28 November 1919.

1920

The Naked Man. [A review of Gardner's *William Blake the Man*]. *Athenaeum*, 13 February 1920.

The Phoenix Society. [A letter] To the Editor. *Athenaeum*, 27 February 1920.

A Brief Treatise on the Criticism of Poetry. *Chapbook*, March 1920.

Dante as a 'Spiritual Leader.' *Athenaeum*, 2 April 1920.

The Poetic Drama. *Athenaeum*, 14 May 1920.

The Old Comedy. *Athenaeum*, 11 June 1920.

The Perfect Critic. [A letter] To the Editor. *Athenaeum*, 6 August 1920.

'The Duchess of Malfi' at the Lyric and Poetic Drama. *Art and Letters*, Winter 1920.

The Second Order Mind. *Dial*, December 1920.

1921

London Letter. *Dial*, April-December 1921.

Prose and Verse. *Chapbook*, April 1921.

1922

London Letter. *Dial*, January-December 1922.

Lettre d'Angleterre. *Nouvelle Revue Francaise*, 1 May, 1 December 1922.

The Three Provincialities. *Tyro*, No. 2, 1922.

1923

Dramatis Personae. *Criterion*, April 1923.

Ben Jonson. *Nation and Athenaeum*, 30 June 1923.

The Function of a Literary Review. *Criterion*, July 1923.

Andrew Marvell. *Nation and Athenaeum*, 29 September 1923.

Beating a Drum. *Nation and Athenaeum*, 6 October 1923.

T. S. Eliot

The Classics in France and in England. *Criterion*, October 1923.
Lettre d'Angleterre. *Nouvelle Revue Francaise*, 1 November 1923.
Ulysses Order and Myth. *Dial*, November 1923.
Marianne Moore. *Dial*, December 1923.

1924

Communication [to the Editor]. *Transatlantic Review*, January 1924.
[A review of] 'The Growth of Civilization and the Origin of Magic and Religion', by W. J. Perry. *Criterion*, July 1924.

1925

On the Eve. A Dialogue. *Criterion*, January 1925.
Rencontre. *Nouvelle Revue Francaise*, 1 April 1925.
The Ballet. *Criterion*, April 1925.

1926

The Idea of a Literary Review. *Criterion*, January 1926.
Mr Robertson and Mr Shaw. *Criterion*, April 1926.
[A review of] 'All God's Chillun got Wings', 'Desire under the Elms', and 'Welded', by Eugene O'Neill. *Criterion*, April 1926.
Mr Read and Mr Fernandez. *Criterion*, October 1926.
Note sur Mallarmé et Poe. *Nouvelle Revue Francaise*, November 1926.
Whitman and Tennyson. *Nation and Athenaeum*, 18 December 1926.

1927

Grammar and Usage. *Criterion*, January 1927.
Homage to Wilkie Collins. *Criterion*, January 1927.
A Note on Poetry and Belief. *Enemy*, January 1927.
Literature, Science and Dogma. *Dial*, March 1927.
Le Roman Anglais Contemporain. *Nouvelle Revue Francaise*, 1 May 1927.
Poet and Saint. *Dial*, May 1927.
Popular Theologians: Mr Wells, Mr Belloc and Mr Murry. *Criterion*, May 1927.
Recent Detective Fiction, *Criterion*, June 1927.
Political Theorists, *Criterion*, July 1927.
Why Mr Russell is a Christian. *Criterion*, August 1927.
The Silurist. *Dial*, September 1927.
The Mysticism of William Blake. *Nation and Athenaeum*, 17 September 1927.
Mr Middleton Murry's Synthesis. *Criterion*, October 1927.
Bradley's Ethical Studies. *Times Literary Supplement*, 29 December 1927.
Deux Attitudes Mystiques: Dante et Donne. *Le Roseau d'or*. *Troisième Numero de Chroniques*, 1927.

Check List

1928

Isolated Superiority. *Dial*, January 1928.

An Emotional Unity. *Dial*, February 1928.

The *Action Francaise*, M. Maurras and Mr Ward. *Criterion*, March 1928.

A Reply to Mr Ward. *Criterion*, June 1928.

Mr Lucas's Webster. *Criterion*, June 1928.

The Oxford Jonson. *Dial*, July 1928.

The Golden Ass of Apuleius. *Dial*, September 1928.

Civilization: 1928 Model. *Criterion*, September 1928.

Freud's Illusions. *Criterion*, December 1928.

The Literature of Fascism. *Criterion*, December 1928.

The Idealism of Julien Benda. *The Cambridge Review*, 6 June 1928. Reprinted in *The New Republic*, 12 December 1928.

1929

Introduction to Goethe. *Nation and Athenaeum*, 12 January 1929.

Contemporary Literature. Is Modern Realism Frankness or Filth? *Forum*, February 1929.

Sherlock Holmes and his Times. *Criterion*, April 1929.

A Letter [to the Editor]. *Little Review*, May 1929.

Mr Barnes and Mr Rowse. *Criterion*, July 1929.

1930

[A review of] 'Baudelaire and the Symbolists', by Peter Quennell. *Criterion*, January 1930.

[A review of] 'God: Being an introduction to the Science of Metabiology', by J. Middleton Murry. *Criterion*, January 1930.

Poetry and Propaganda. [American] *Bookman*, February 1930.

1931

[A review of] 'Son of Woman, The Story of D. H. Lawrence', by J. Middleton Murry. *Criterion*, July 1931.

1932

George Herbert. *Spectator*, 12 March 1932.

1933

Les Caractères Feminins chez Thomas Middleton. *Cahiers du Sud*, June-July 1933.

Housman on Poetry. *Criterion*, October 1933.

1934

'The Rock.' [A letter] to the Editor. *Spectator*, 8 June 1934.

[A review of] 'The Mystical Doctrine of St John of the Cross'. *Criterion*, July 1934. Ascribed to T. S. Eliot in index.

What does the Church stand for? *Spectator*, 19 August 1934.

T. S. Eliot

1935

Dowson's Poems. *Times Literary Supplement*, 10 January 1935.

Views and Reviews. *New English Weekly*, 6 June, 20 June, 12 September and 7 November 1935.

Literature and the Modern World. *American Prefaces*, November 1935.

Audiences, Producers, Plays, Poets. *New Verse*, December 1935.

1936

Mr Reckitt, Mr Tomlin and the Crisis. *New English Weekly*, 25 February 1936.

Note on a Recent Correspondence. *New English Weekly*, 19 March 1936.

[A review of] 'Shakespeare', by J. Middleton Murry. *Criterion*, July 1936.

1937

[A review of] 'The Lion and the Fox', by Wyndham Lewis. *Twentieth Century Verse*, November-December 1937.

1938

On a Recent Piece of Criticism. *Purpose*, April-June 1938.
Criticizes an article by G. W. Stonier on Ezra Pound.

Five Points on Dramatic Writing. *Townsman*, July 1938.

1939

A Commentary. *New English Weekly*, 27 April, 11 May, 5 October 1939.

A Sub-Pagan Society? *New English Weekly*. 14 December 1939.

1940

Views and Reviews. *New English Weekly*, 8 February, 15 February, 19 December 1940.

The Poetry of W. B. Yeats. *Purpose*, July, December 1940. Also in *The Southern Review*.

[A review of] 'Hopousia'. *Purpose*, July-December 1940.

The Christian News Letter, Nos. 42-43-44. 14, 21, 28 August 1940.
Written by T. S. Eliot in the absence of the editor J. H. Oldham.

A Commentary. *New English Weekly*, 5 December 1940.

1941

A Message to the Fish. *Horizon*, March 1941.
A letter on Joyce.

Virginia Woolf. *Horizon*, May 1941.

Views and Reviews. *New English Weekly*, 26 June 1941.

Check List

1942

A letter to the Editors. *Partisan Review*, March, April 1942.
 A statement on Van Wyck Brooks's lecture: 'Primary Literature and Coterie Literature'.
Planning and Religion. *Theology*, May 1942.
The Christian News Letter, No. 141. 8 July 1942.
 Written by T. S. Eliot in the absence of the editor J. H. Oldham.

1943

Notes Towards a Definition of Culture. *New English Weekly*, 21 January, 28 January, 4 February and 11 February 1943. Reprinted in *Partisan Review*, Spring 1944.
The Social Function of Poetry. *Norseman*, November 1943. French version in *Poésie 45*. Reprinted in *The Adelphi*, July-September 1945.
Message [to the Editor]. *Aguedal* (Rabat, Morocco), Nos. 3-4, December 1943.

1944

The Responsibility of the Man of Letters in the Cultural Restoration of Europe. *Norseman*, July-August 1944. Reprinted in *Horizon*, December 1944 and *The Sewanee Review*, Summer 1945.
What is Minor Poetry? *Welsh Review*, December 1944. Reprinted in *The Sewanee Review*, Winter 1946.

1945

T. S. Eliot on the Condition of Man Today. [An interview with J. P. Hodin] *Horizon*, August 1945.
Cultural Diversity and European Unity. *Review 45*, 11 (1945): Allen and Unwin, London.
The Class and the Elite. *New English Review*, October 1945.

TRANSLATIONS

Concerning 'Intuition', by Charles Mauron. *Criterion*, September 1927.
Prologue to an Essay on Criticism, by Charles Maurras. [1-11]. *Criterion*, January, March 1928.
On reading Einstein, by Charles Mauron. *Criterion*, October 1930.

This book is set in 12-pt. Perpetua, a type-face originally cut in Hoptonwood stone in 1927 by the sculptor, typographer, and wood-engraver Eric Gill. The matrices for Perpetua were cut by the Monotype Corporation in 1934. Its accompanying italic is closely related to the roman letter and is often referred to as an oblique roman, being less sloped than most other italic type-faces. The value of the Perpetua type family lies in its light appearance, clean cut, and its complete lack of ornamentation. It is a twentieth-century type, still increasing in popularity.

The book has been designed by Henry Jacob